Jazz Standards
FOR SOLO GUITAR

ISBN 0-634-02878-2

HAL•LEONARD®
CORPORATION
7777 W. BLUEMOUND RD. P.O. BOX 13819 MILWAUKEE, WI 53213

Visit Hal Leonard Online at
www.halleonard.com

PREFACE

This book contains 35 professional chord melody arrangements for solo guitar. The selections come from some of the finest composers of the 20th century, and are well known by musicians and singers. The book is for guitarists who want to learn chord melody arrangements, new chords, when and how to use them, and when and how to put bass lines within chords. You'll also learn that just because a chord has a long name, it doesn't have to be difficult to play!

Melody, lyrics, and rhythm give a certain feel to a song, but chords have their own personalities that can greatly affect the mood as well. Major seventh chords are beautiful; dominant ninth chords are bluesy; minor ninth chords are dark and soulful; diminished chords build tension; augmented chords sound mysterious; major 6/9th chords sound bright and happy; dominant 7#9 chords sound bold and exciting. A minor ninth chord with a major seventh or a sharp eleventh can add drama to an ending—so can a major seventh.

Through my choice of chords I have tried to enhance the feel of a song. For instance, I have tried to make pretty songs beautiful by using major seventh chords. Conversely, for sad songs, I have used dramatic, brooding chords.

It is my great desire that the study of this book helps you in making your own chord melody arrangements. When one arranges a song and makes it one's own, it is a very satisfying feeling and gives a sense of pride and accomplishment.

—Robert B. Yelin

DEDICATION

This book is dedicated to my first guitar teacher, Gus DeGazio, who made me aware of the inherent beauty of the sound of guitar chords from Johnny Smith records. This book is also dedicated to the premier guitarist, Johnny Smith, who has no equal in revealing the beauty of the guitar. Though he was never my teacher, his playing is the reason I play guitar. I strive for his beauty and to reap the rewards that dedication and hard work bring. I am also very blessed to have Gus and Johnny as two, very dear, loving friends.

Ain't Misbehavin'

from AIN'T MISBEHAVIN'

Words by Andy Razaf
Music by Thomas "Fats" Waller and Harry Brooks

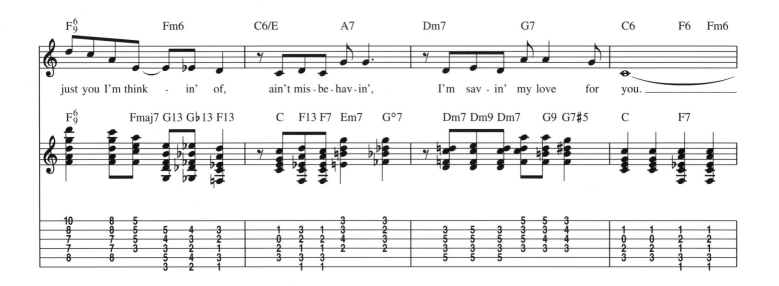

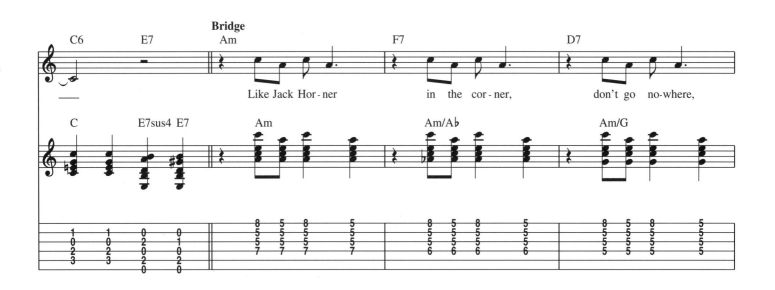

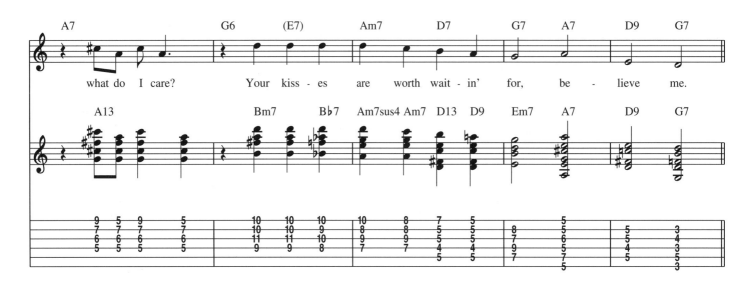

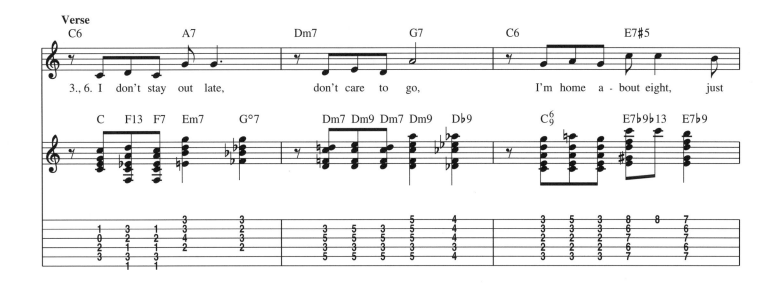

Verse

3., 6. I don't stay out late,   don't care to go,   I'm home a-bout eight,   just

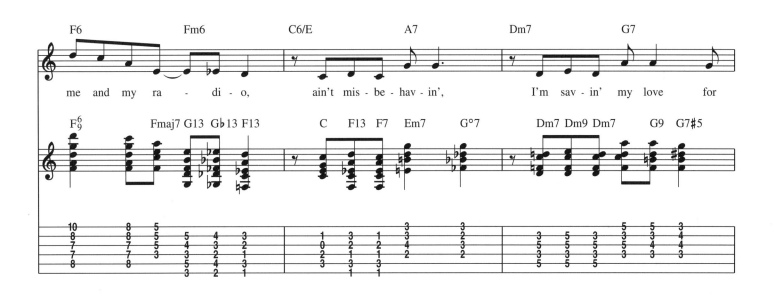

me and my ra - di - o,   ain't mis - be - hav - in',   I'm sav - in' my love   for

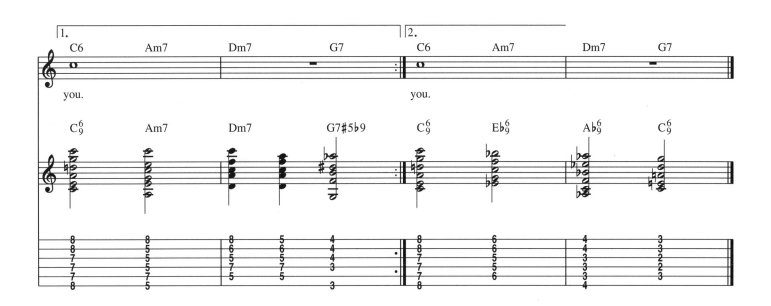

1.   you.

2.   you.

Autumn Leaves
(Les Feuilles Mortes)

English lyric by Johnny Mercer
French lyric by Jacques Prevert
Music by Joseph Kosma

The fall-ing leaves _____ drift by the win-dow, _____ the au-tumn

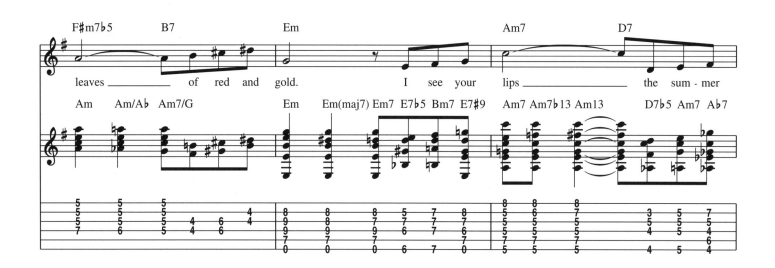

leaves _____ of red and gold. I see your lips _____ the sum-mer

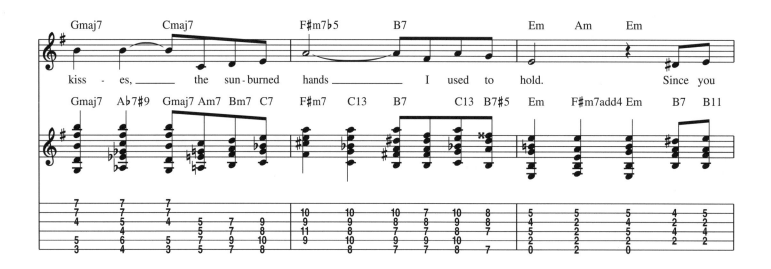

kiss-es, _____ the sun-burned hands _____ I used to hold. Since you

Bewitched

from PAL JOEY

Words by Lorenz Hart
Music by Richard Rodgers

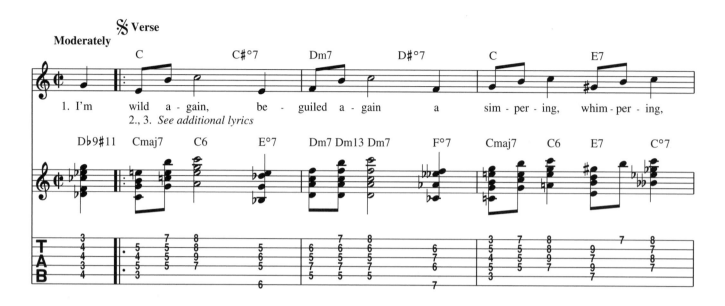

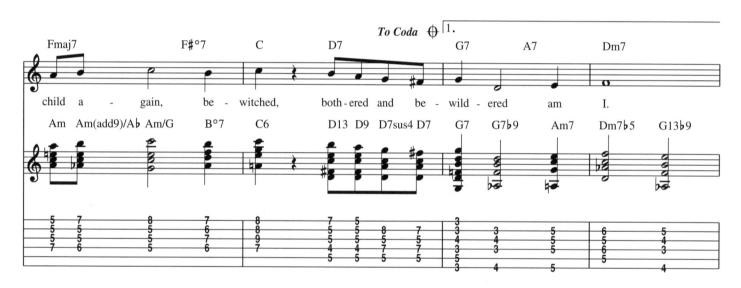

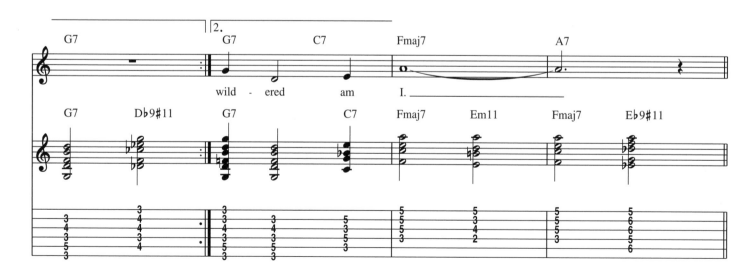

Bridge

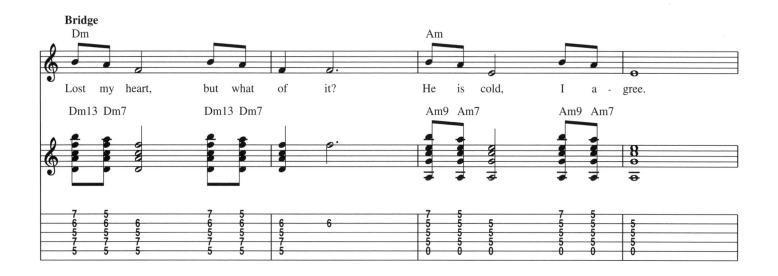

D.S. al Coda

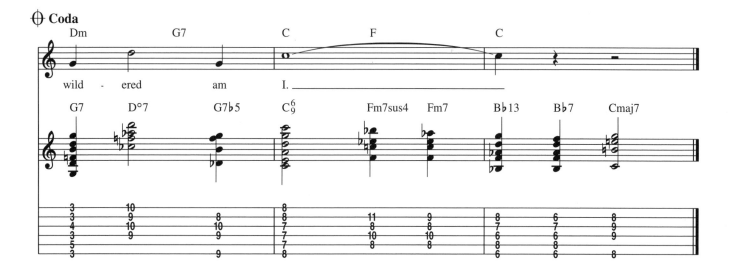

Additional Lyrics

2. Couldn't sleep, and wouldn't sleep,
   When love came and told me I shouldn't sleep.
   Bewitched, bothered and bewildered am I.

3. I'll sing to him, each spring to him,
   And long for the day when I'll cling to him.
   Bewitched, bothered and bewildered am I.

But Beautiful

Words by Johnny Burke
Music by Jimmy Van Heusen

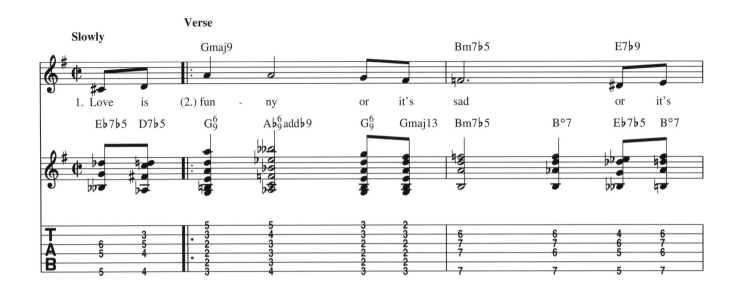

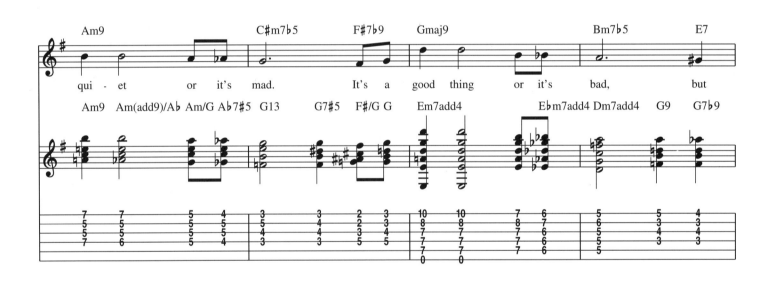

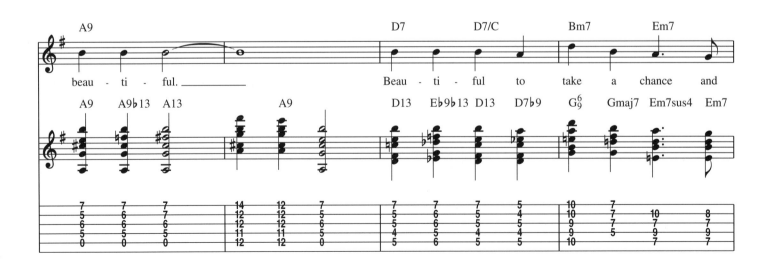

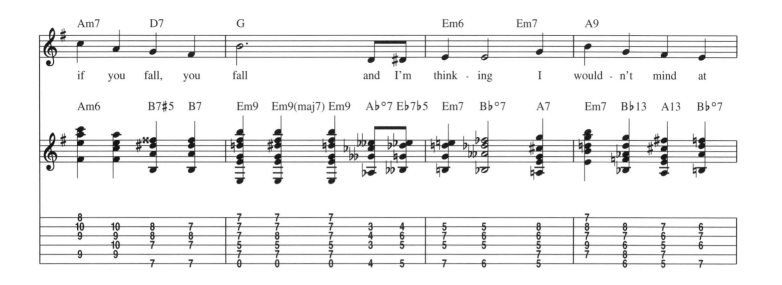

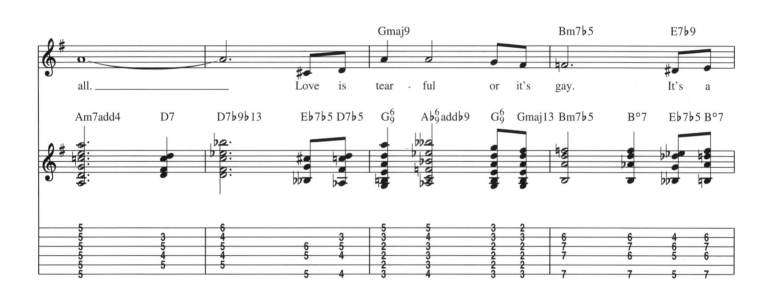

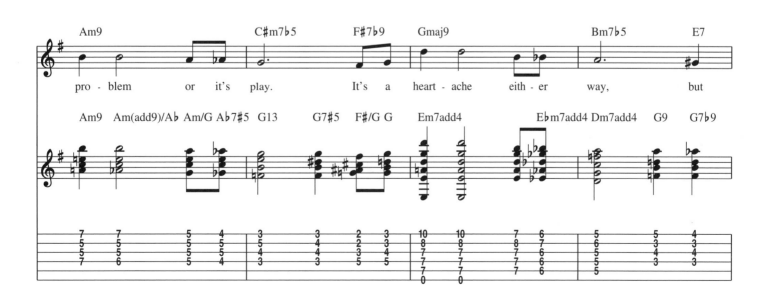

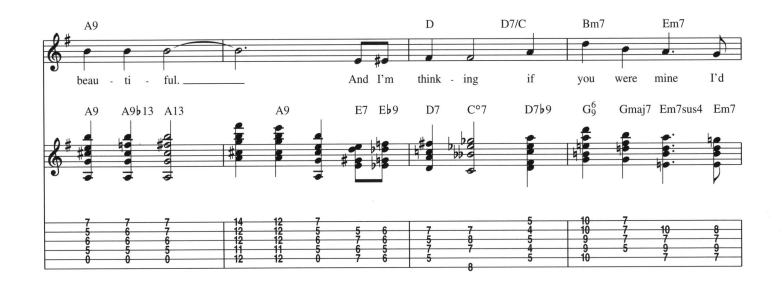

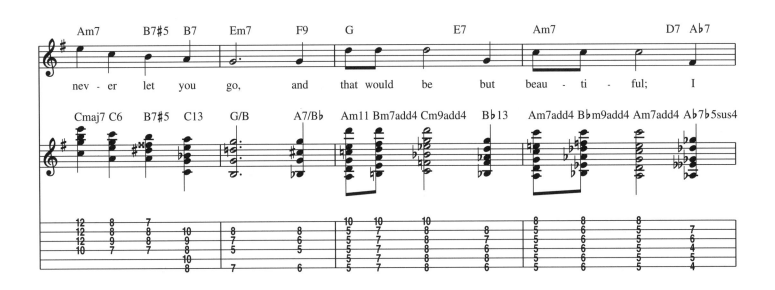

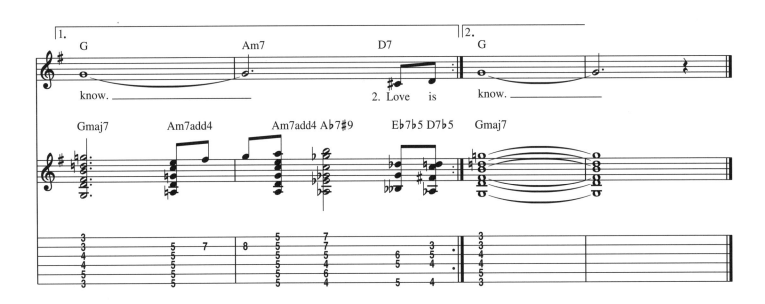

Cherokee
(Indian Love Song)

Words and Music by Ray Noble

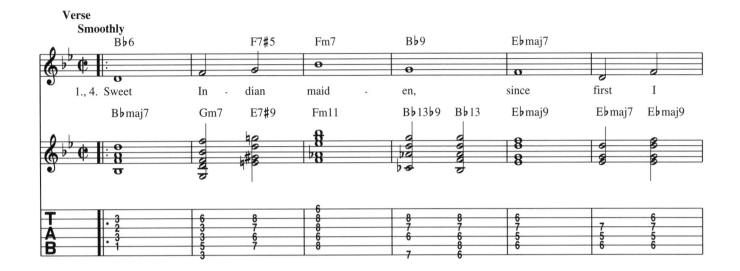

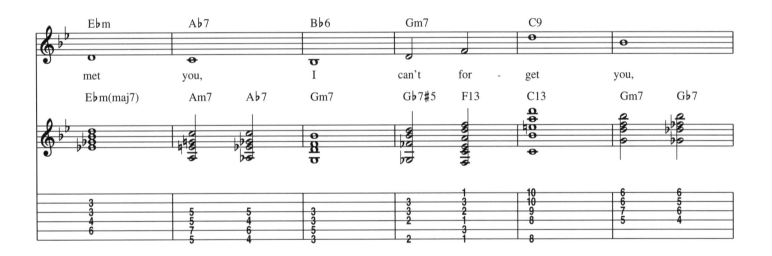

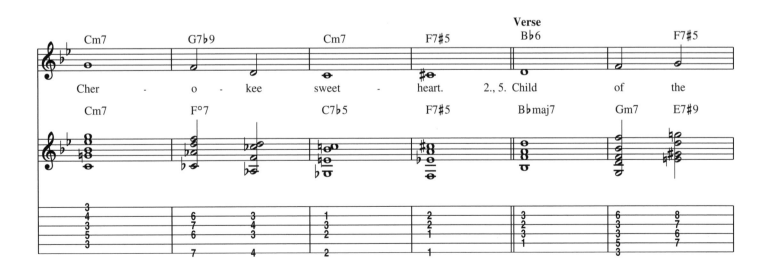

Darn That Dream

Lyric by Eddie De Lange
Music by Jimmy Van Heusen

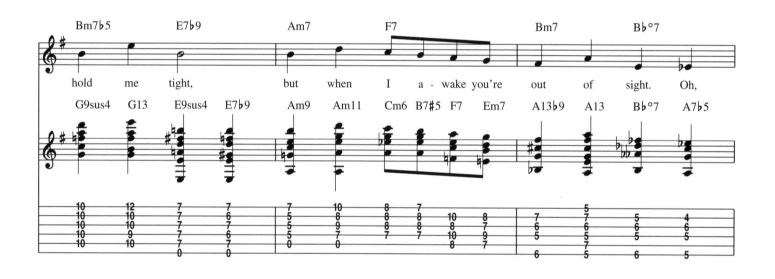

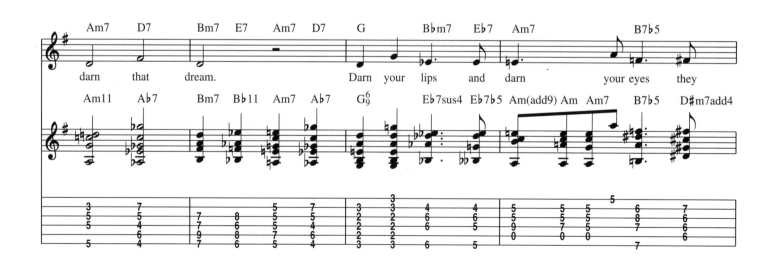

Verse

2. Darn that dream and bless it too, with-out that dream I nev - er

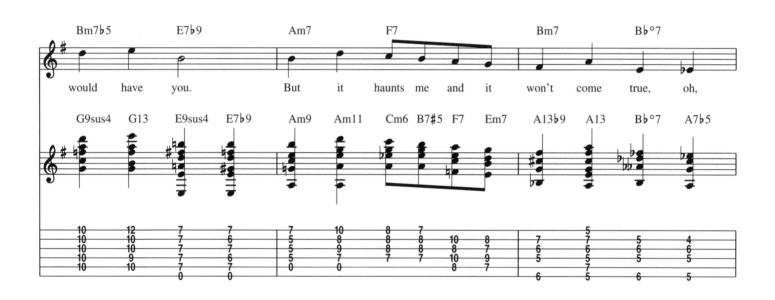

would have you. But it haunts me and it won't come true, oh,

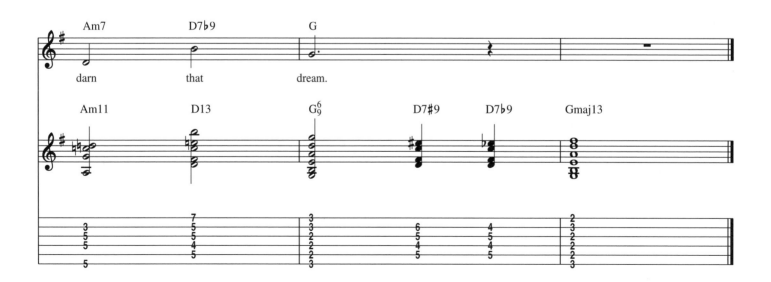

darn that dream.

A Day in the Life of a Fool
(Manha De Carnaval)

Words by Carl Sigman
Music by Luiz Bonfa

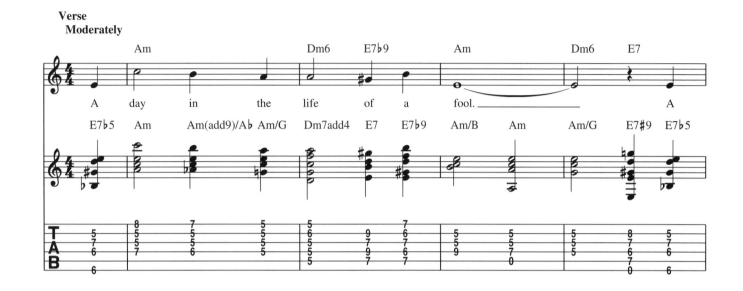

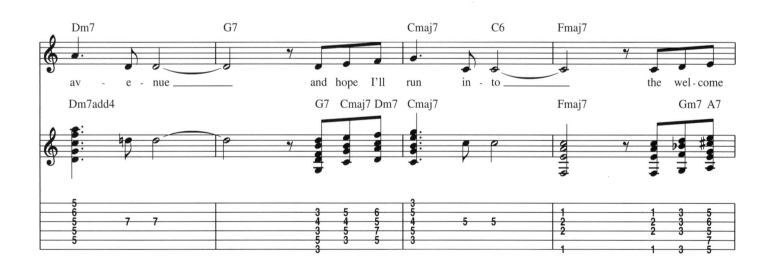

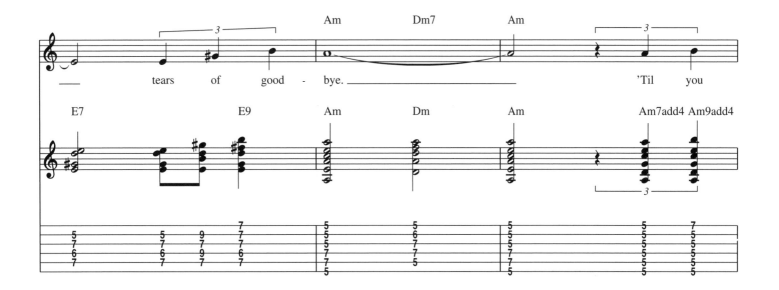

tears of good - bye. 'Til you

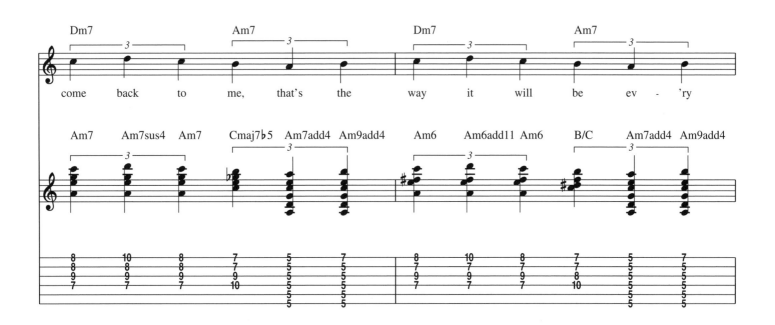

come back to me, that's the way it will be ev - 'ry

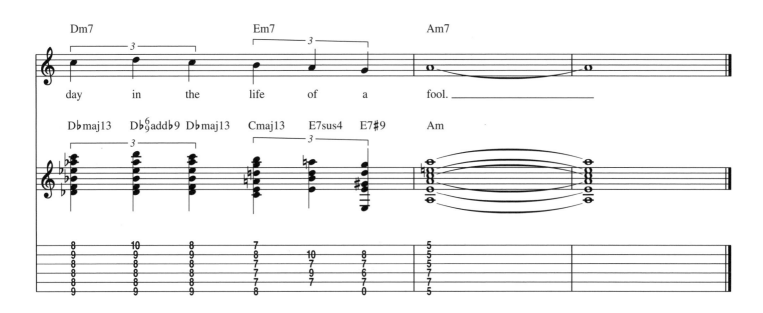

day in the life of a fool.

Falling in Love With Love

from THE BOYS FROM SYRACUSE

Words by Lorenz Hart
Music by Richard Rodgers

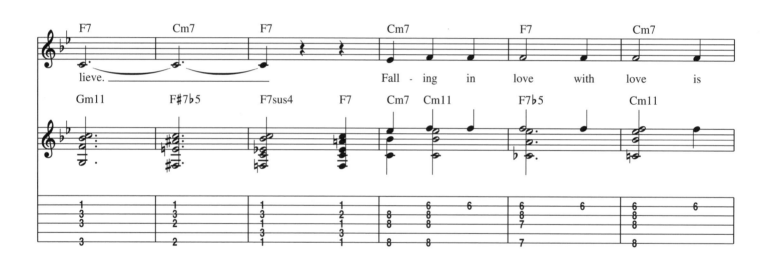

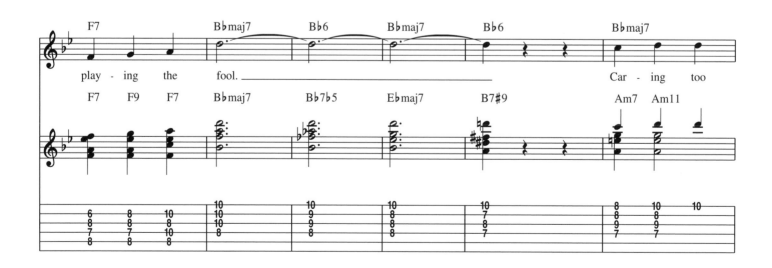

Girl Talk

from the Paramount Picture HARLOW

Words by Bobby Troup
Music by Neal Hefti

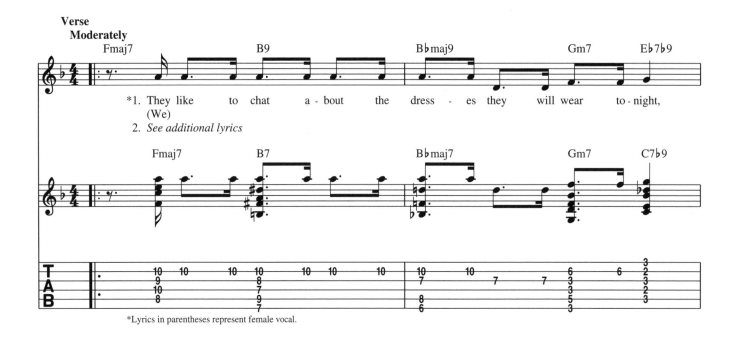

*1. They like to chat a-bout the dress-es they will wear to-night,
(We)
2. *See additional lyrics*

*Lyrics in parentheses represent female vocal.

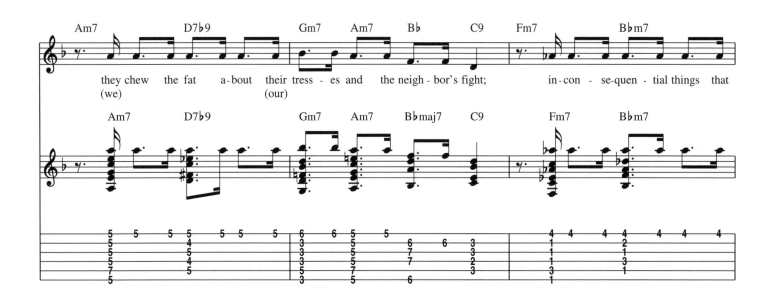

they chew the fat a-bout their tress-es and the neigh-bor's fight;
(we) (our)
in-con-se-quen-tial things that

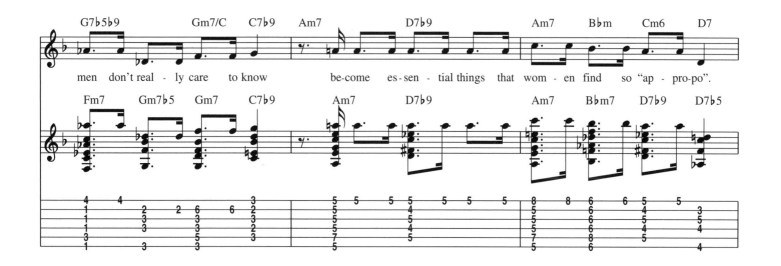

men don't real - ly care to know   be-come es - sen - tial things that wom - en find so "ap - pro-po".

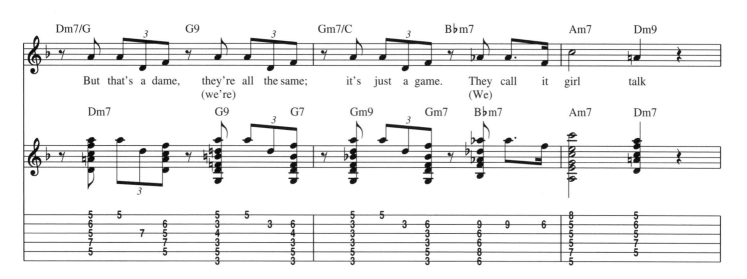

But that's a dame, they're all the same; it's just a game. They call it girl talk
(we're) (We)

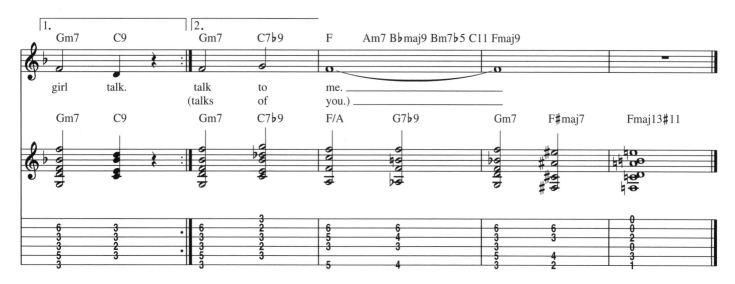

girl talk. talk to me. _____
(talks of you.) _____

Additional Lyrics

2. They all meow about the ups and downs of all their friends,
(We) (our)

The "who," the "how," the "why," they dish the dirt, it never ends.
(we)

The weaker sex, the speaker sex we mortal males behold,
(you)

But though we joke we wouldn't trade you for a ton of gold.

So baby stay and gab away,
(It's all been planned, so take my hand,

But hear me say that after
(Please understand the sweetest

Girl talk, talk to me.
(Girl talk talks of you.)

Have You Met Miss Jones?

from I'D RATHER BE RIGHT

Words by Lorenz Hart
Music by Richard Rodgers

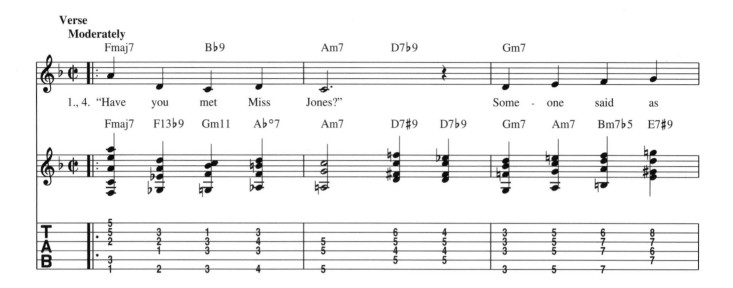

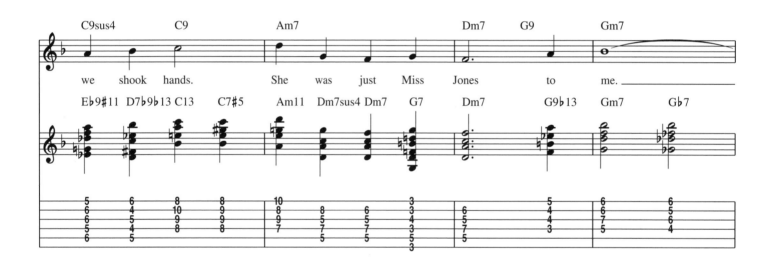

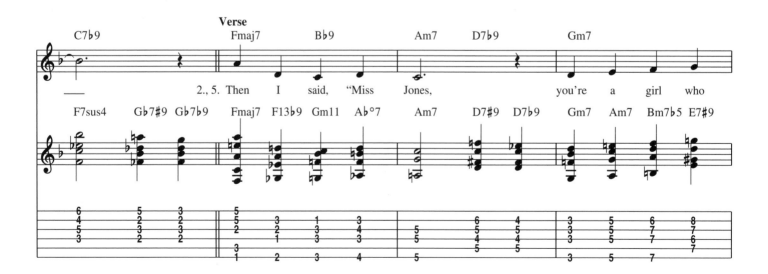

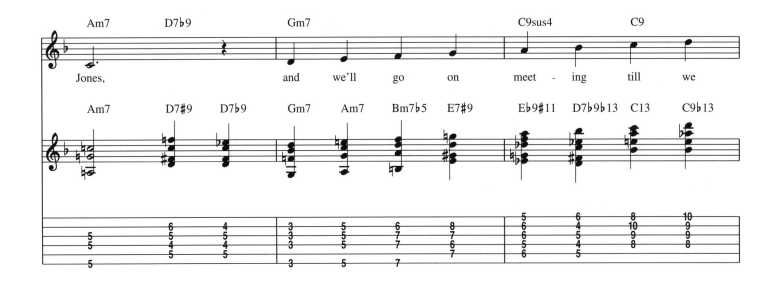

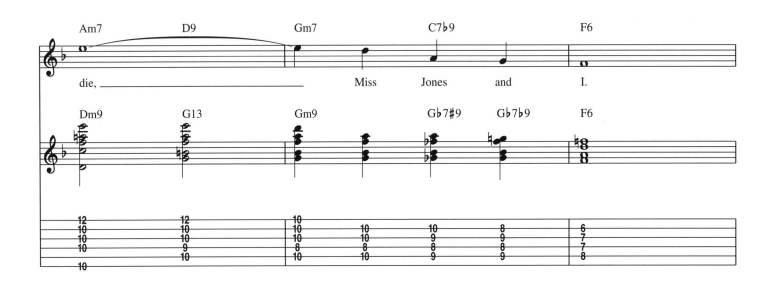

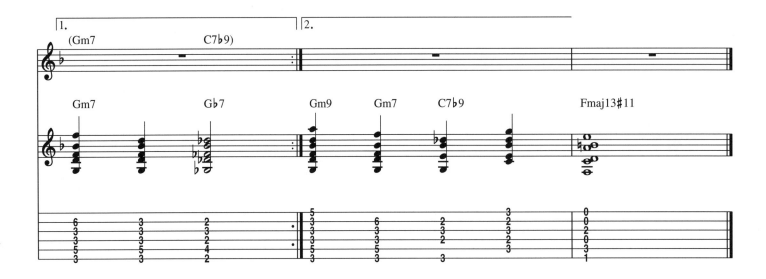

I Got It Bad and That Ain't Good

Words by Paul Francis Webster
Music by Duke Ellington

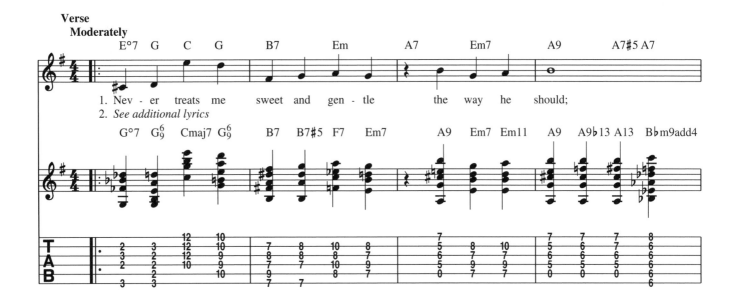

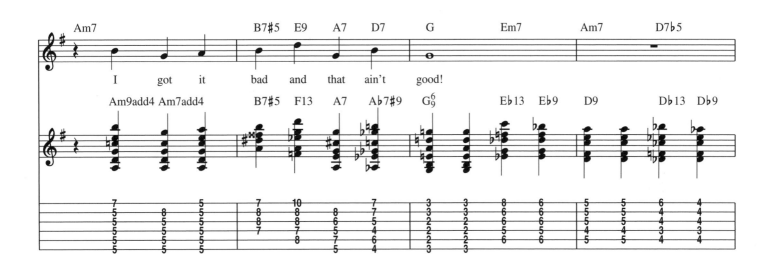

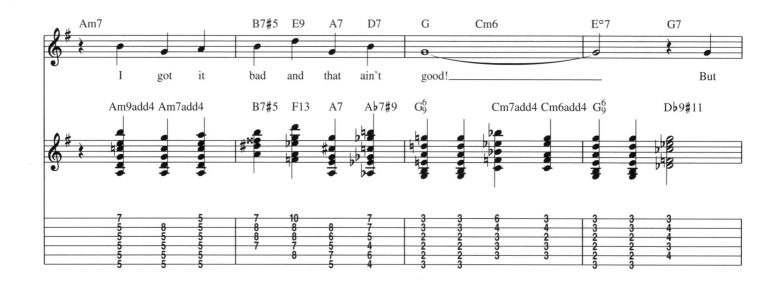

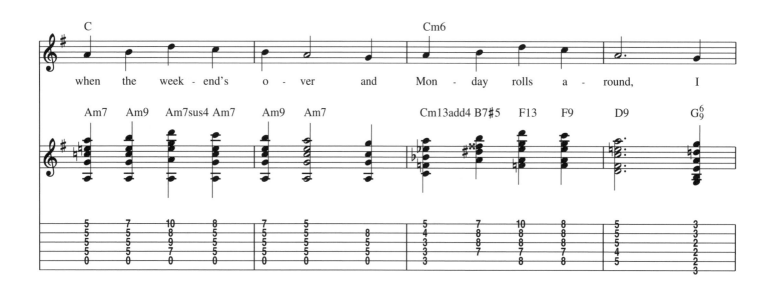

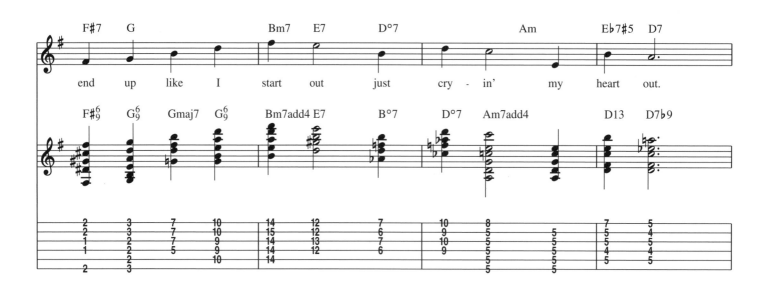

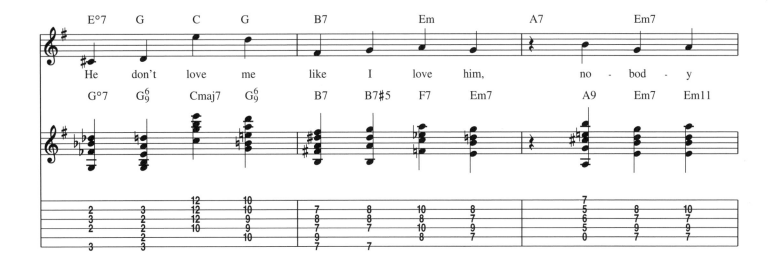

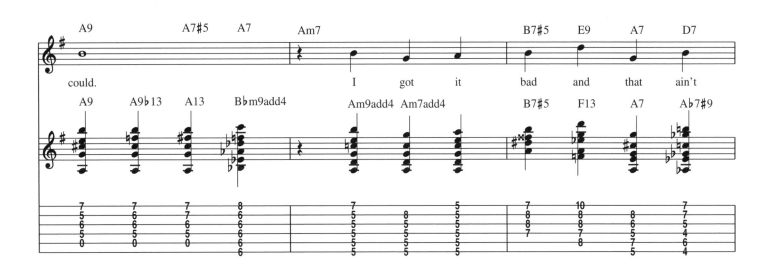

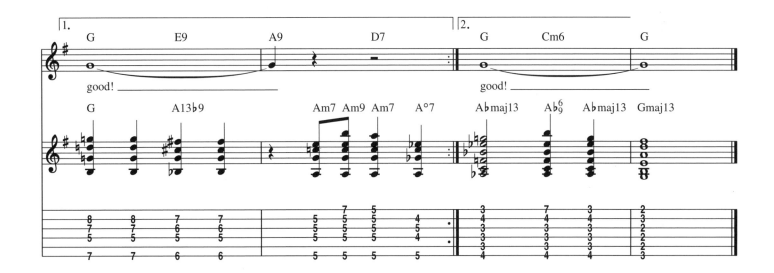

Additional Lyrics

2. Like a lonely weeping willow lost in the wood
I got it bad and that ain't good!
And the things I tell my pillow no woman should.
I got it bad and that ain't good!
Tho folks with good intentions tell me to save my tears
I'm glad I'm mad about him I can't live without him.
Lord above me make him love me the way he should.
I got it bad and that ain't good!

I Hear a Rhapsody

By George Frajos, Jack Baker and Dick Gasparre

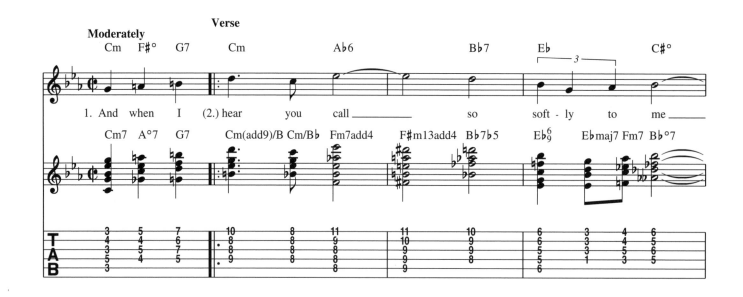

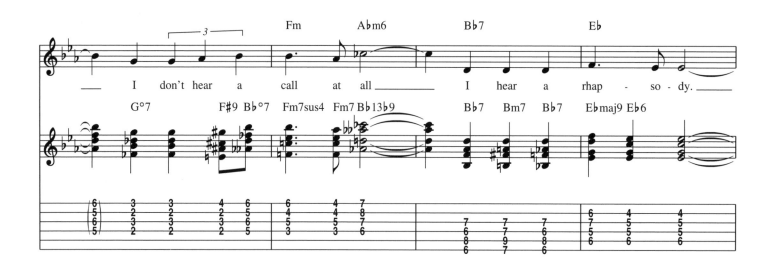

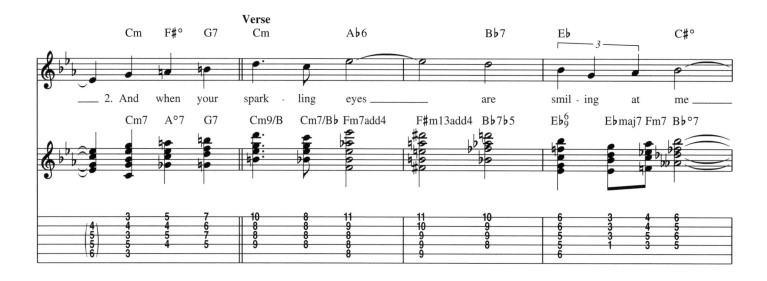

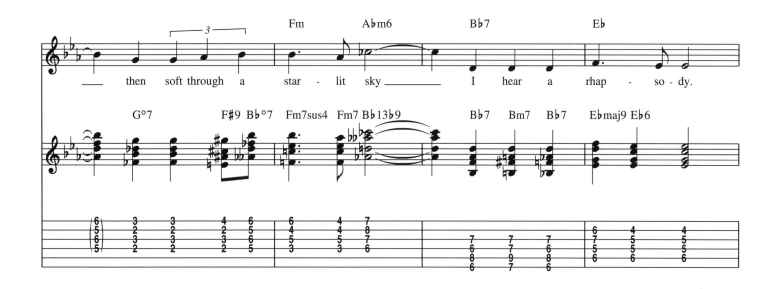

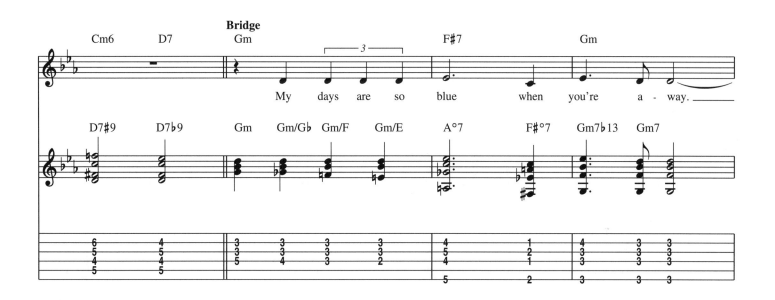

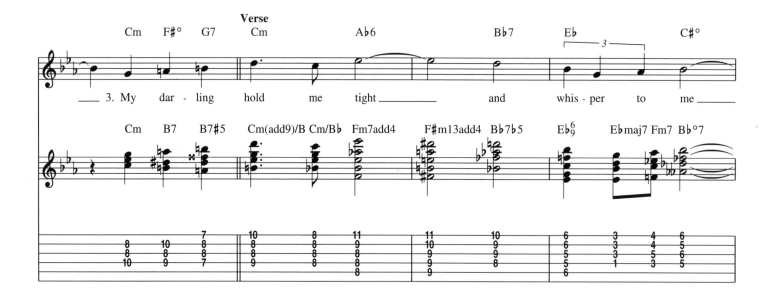

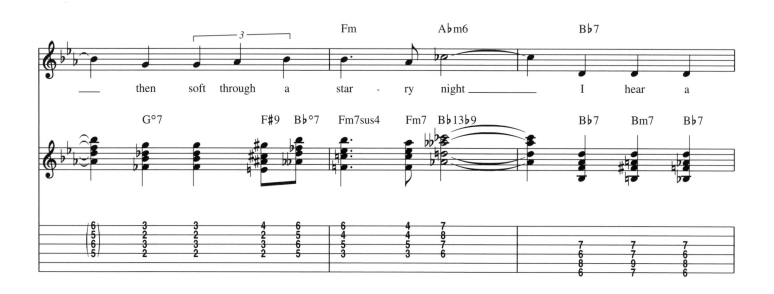

If I Should Lose You

from the Paramount Picture ROSE OF THE RANCHO

Words and Music by Leo Robin and Ralph Rainger

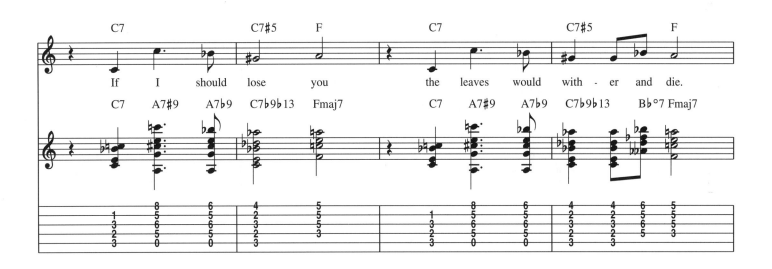

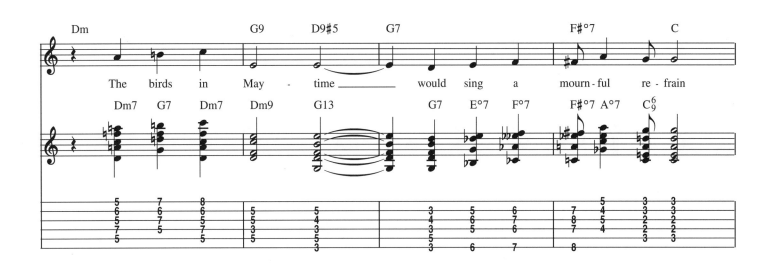

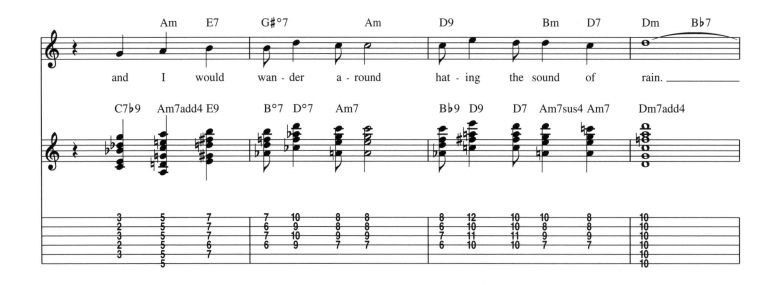

and I would wan - der a - round hat - ing the sound of rain. _____

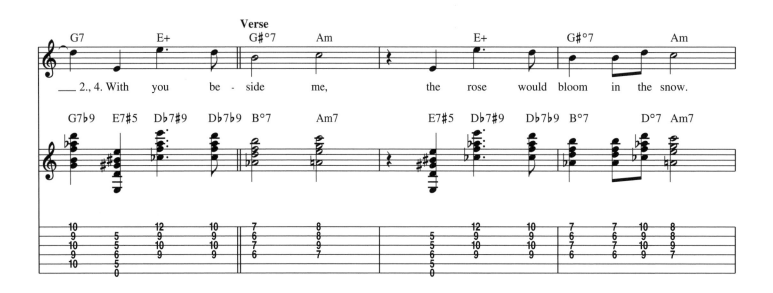

_____ 2., 4. With you be - side me, the rose would bloom in the snow.

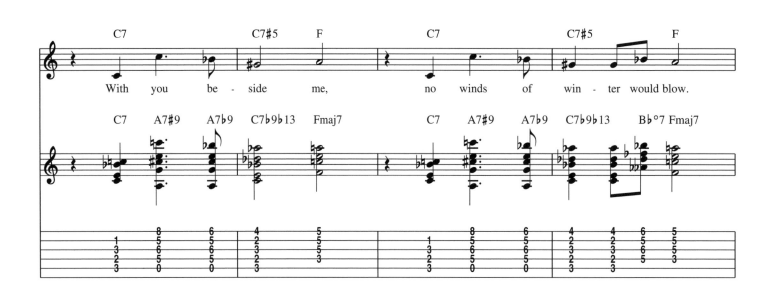

With you be - side me, no winds of win - ter would blow.

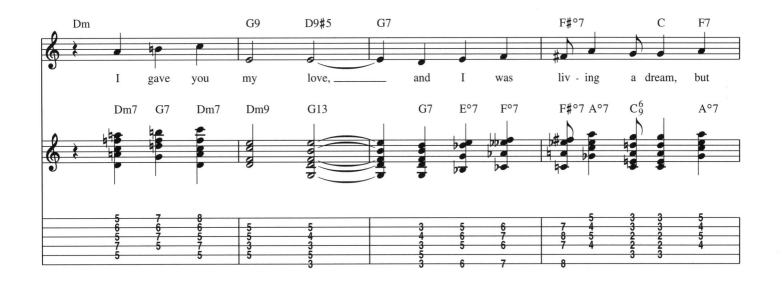

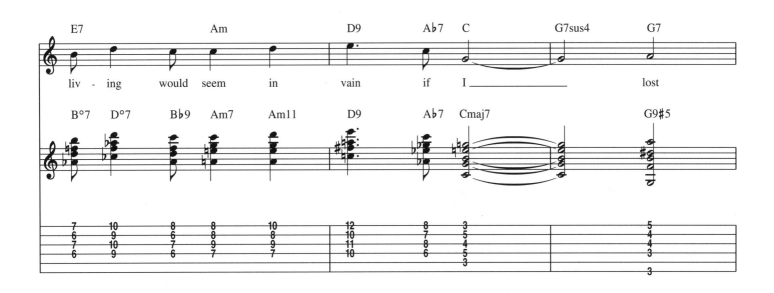

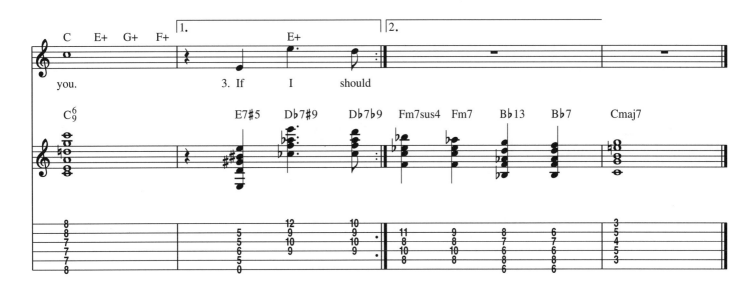

I've Got You Under My Skin

from BORN TO DANCE

Words and Music by Cole Porter

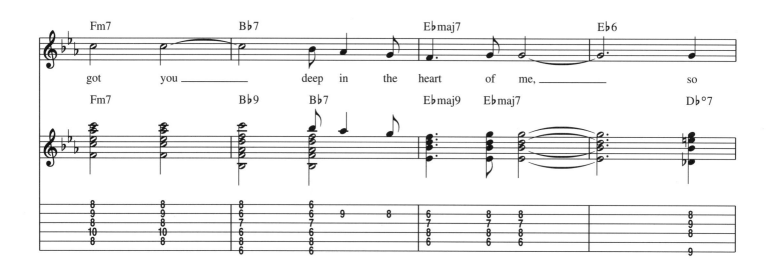

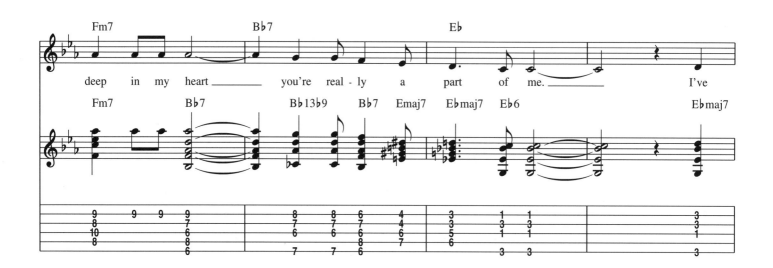

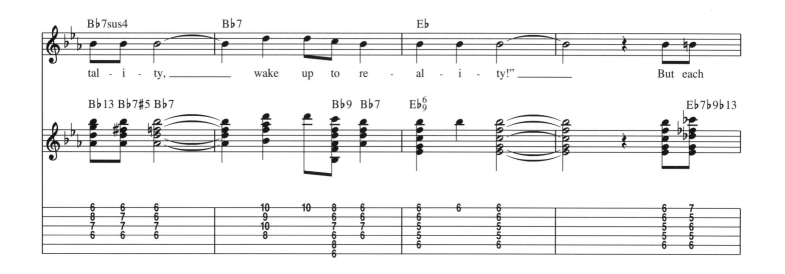

tal - i - ty, _____ wake up to re - al - i - ty!" _____ But each

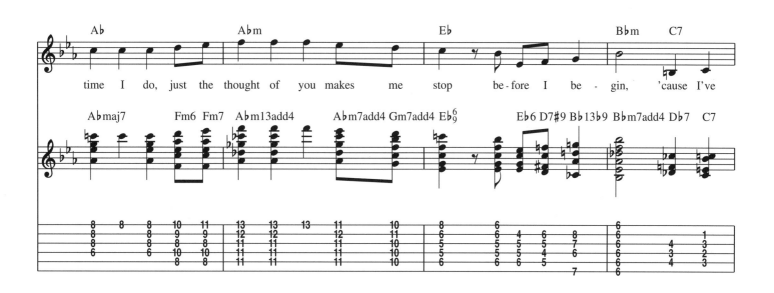

time I do, just the thought of you makes me stop be - fore I be - gin, 'cause I've

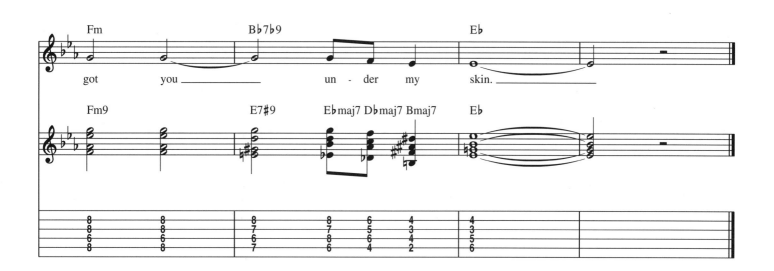

got you _____ un - der my skin. _____

In a Sentimental Mood

Words and Music by Duke Ellington, Irving Mills and Manny Kurtz

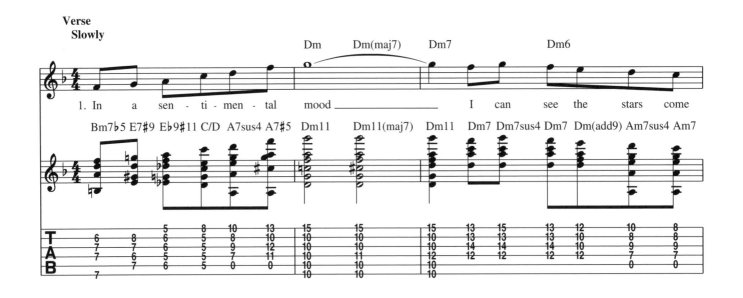

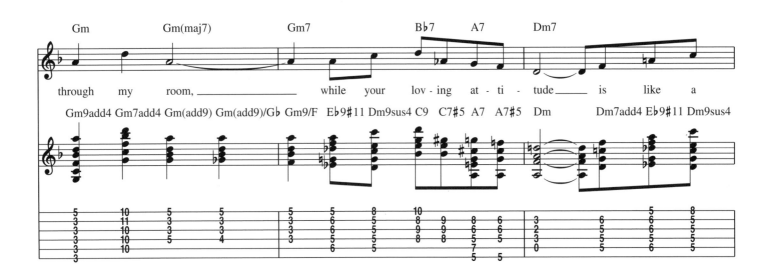

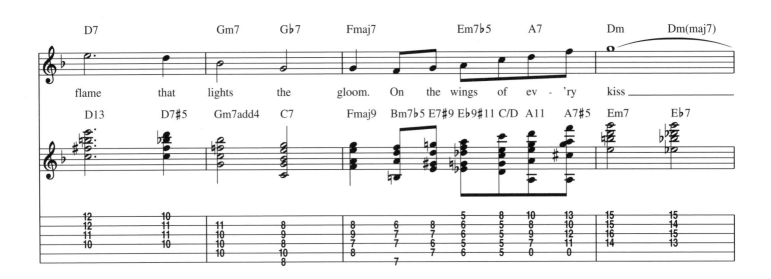

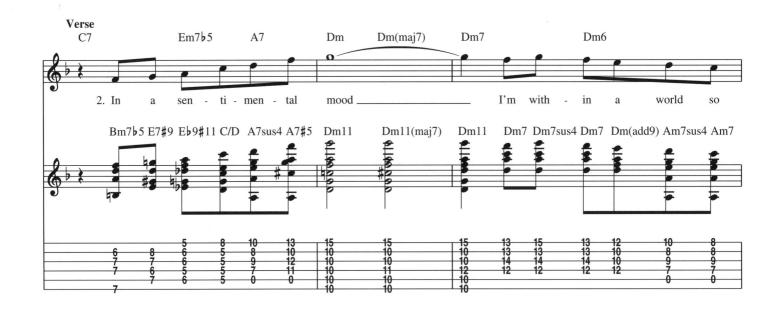

2. In a sen-ti-men-tal mood _____ I'm with-in a world so

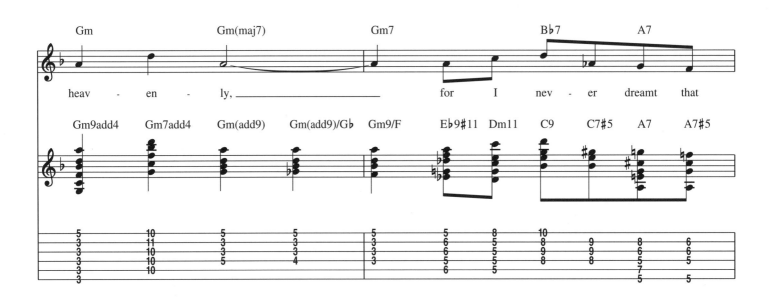

heav-en-ly, _____ for I nev-er dreamt that

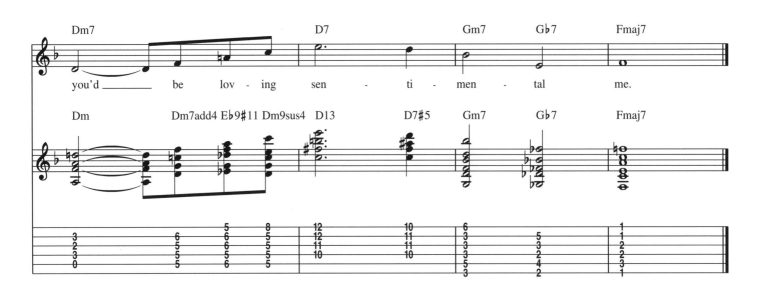

you'd _____ be lov-ing sen-ti-men-tal me.

It Never Entered My Mind

from HIGHER AND HIGHER

Words by Lorenz Hart
Music by Richard Rodgers

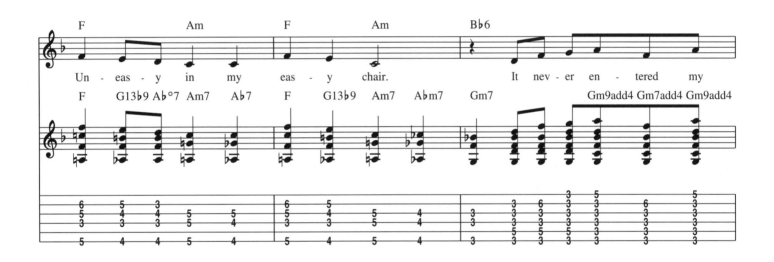

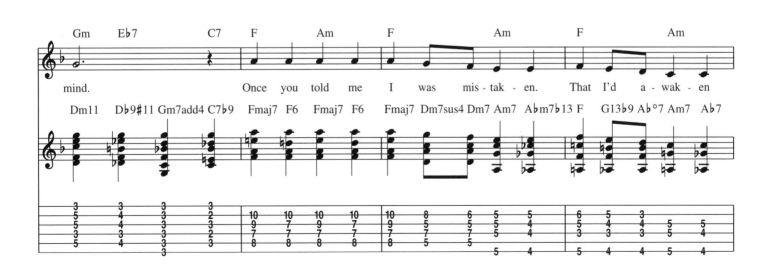

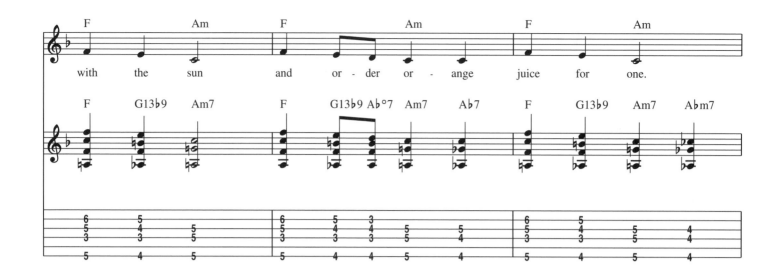

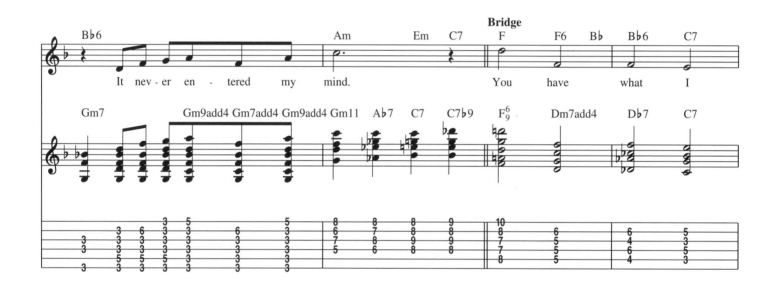

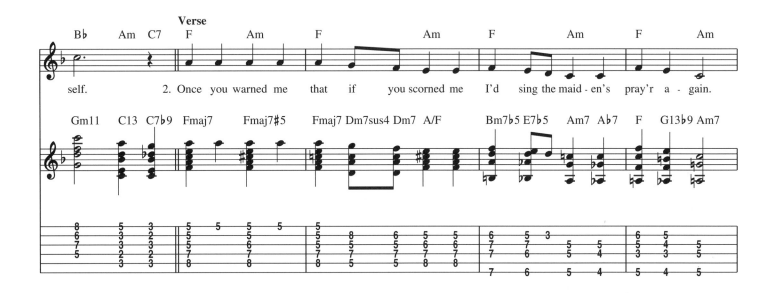

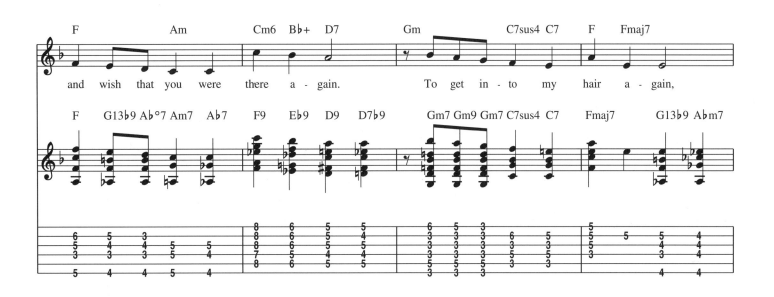

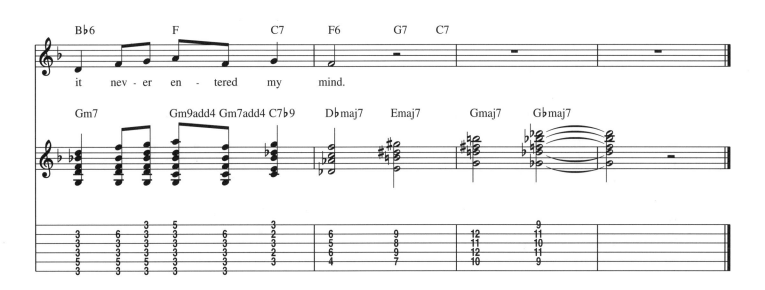

Isn't It Romantic?

from the Paramount Picture LOVE ME TONIGHT

Words by Lorenz Hart
Music by Richard Rodgers

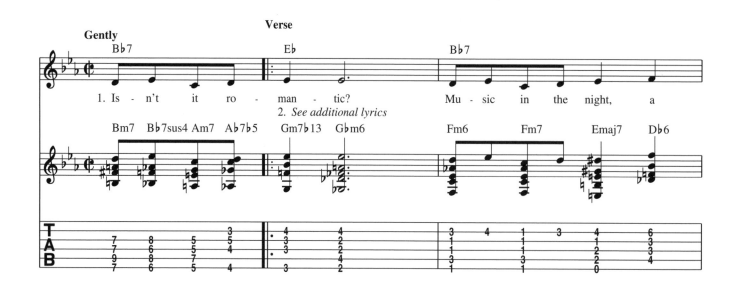

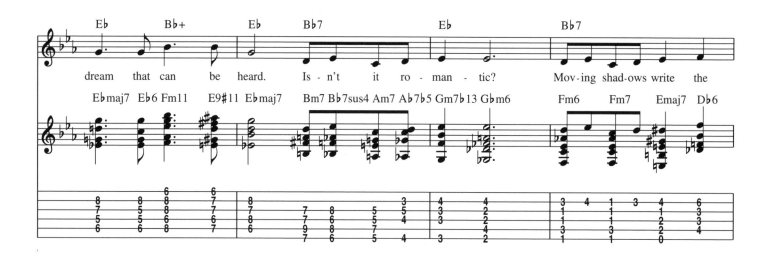

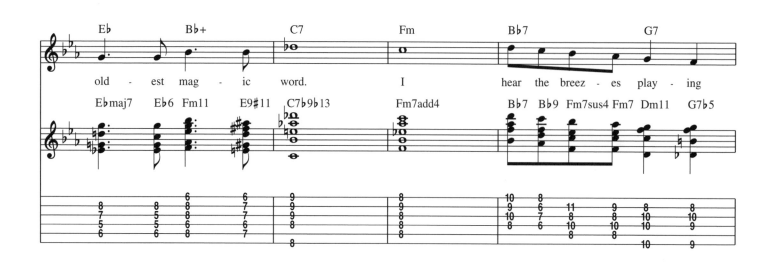

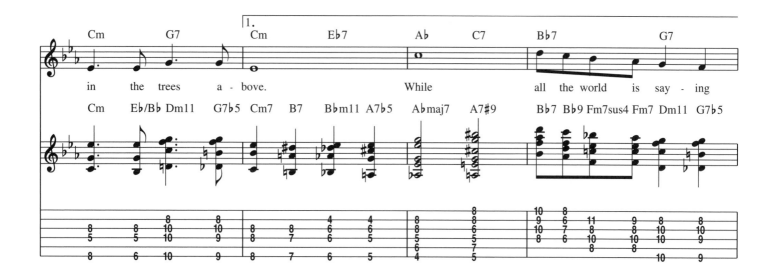

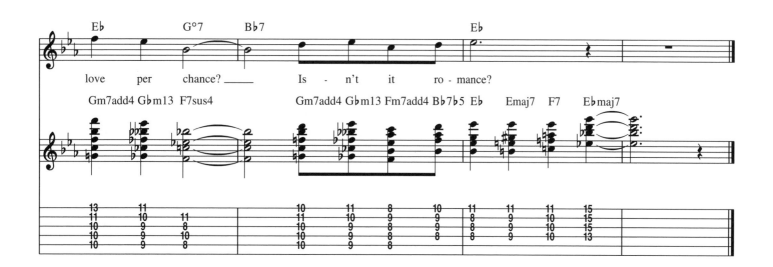

Additional Lyrics

2. Isn't it romantic merely to be young on such a night as this?
Isn't it romantic? Every note that's sung is like a lover's kiss.
Sweet symbols in the moonlight,
Do you mean that I will fall in love per chance?
Isn't it romance?

Like Someone in Love

Words by Johnny Burke
Music by Jimmy Van Heusen

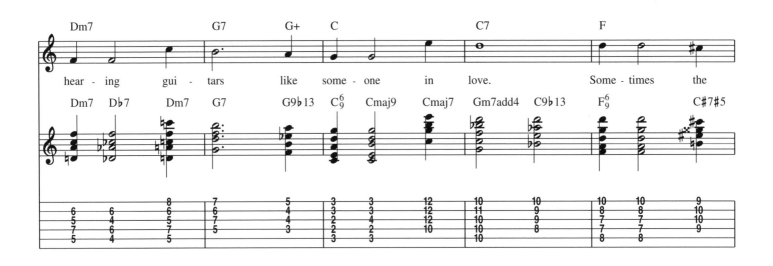

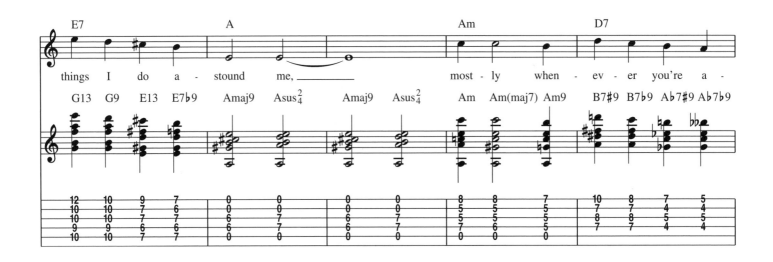

Lullaby of Birdland

Words by George David Weiss
Music by George Shearing

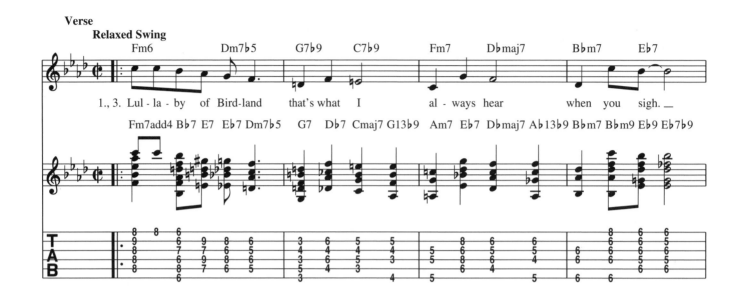

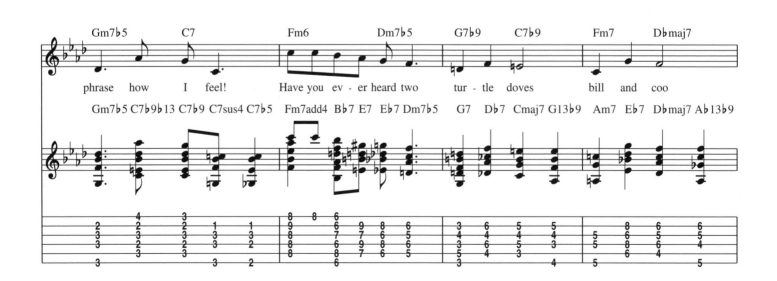

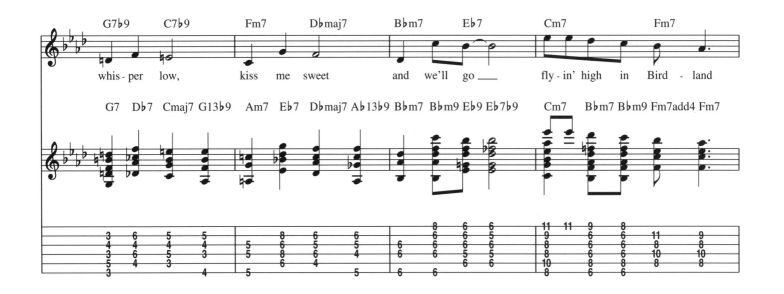

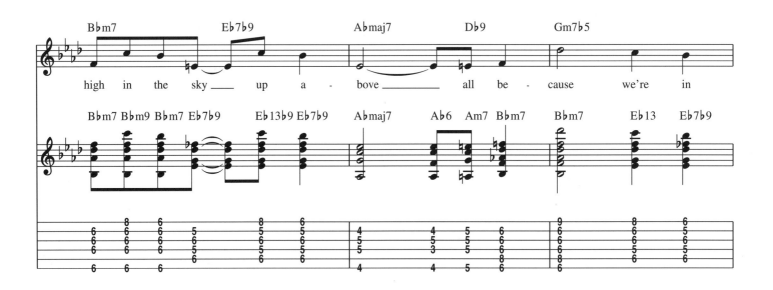

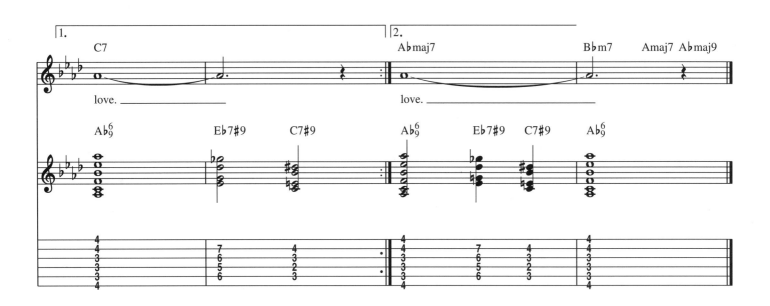

Misty

Words by Johnny Burke
Music by Erroll Garner

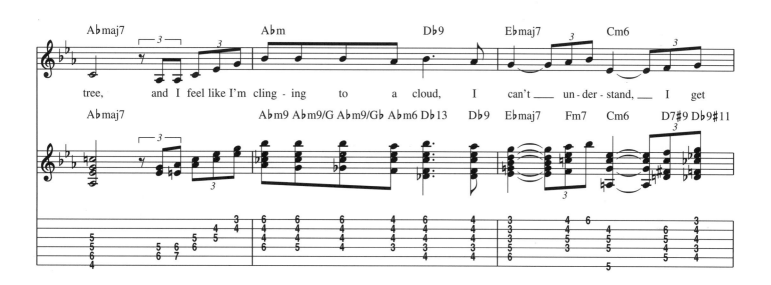

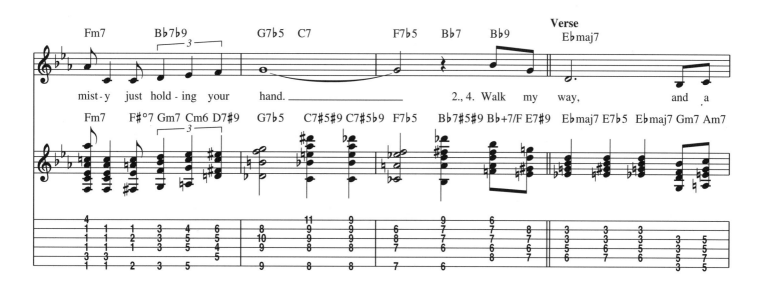

My Favorite Things

from THE SOUND OF MUSIC

Lyrics by Oscar Hammerstein II
Music by Richard Rodgers

1., 4. Rain - drops on ros - es and whisk - ers on kit - tens, bright cop - per
2., 5. *See additional lyrics*

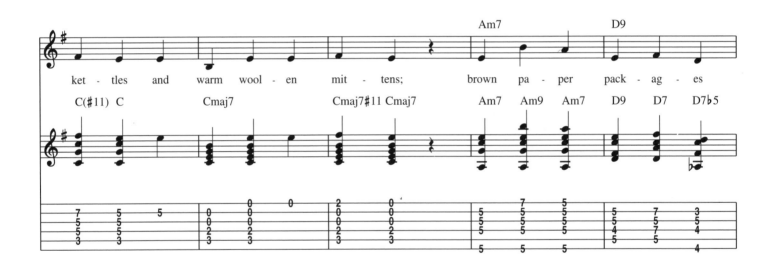

ket - tles and warm wool - en mit - tens; brown pa - per pack - ag - es

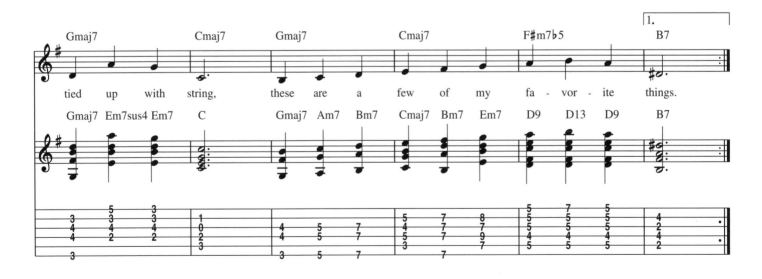

tied up with string, these are a few of my fa - vor - ite things.

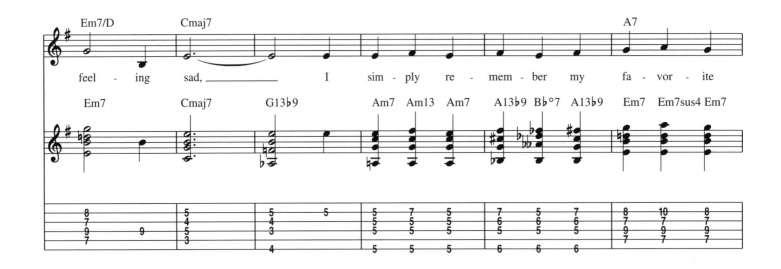

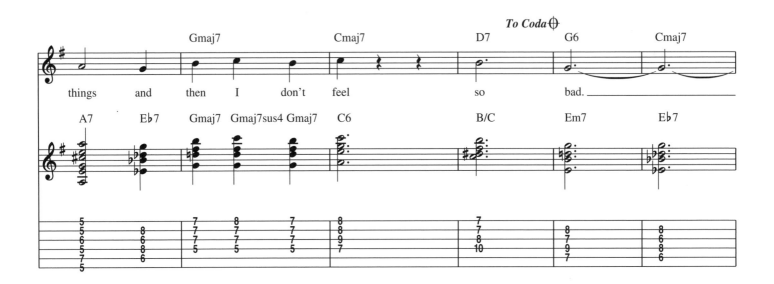

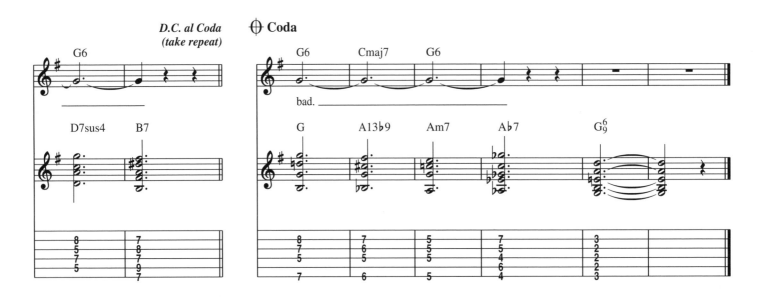

Additional Lyrics

2., 5. Cream-colored ponies and crisp apple strudels,
Doorbells and sleighbells and schnitzel with noodles;
Wild geese that fly with the moon on the wings,
These are a few of my favorite things.

The Nearness of You

from the Paramount Picture ROMANCE IN THE DARK

Words by Ned Washington
Music by Hoagy Carmichael

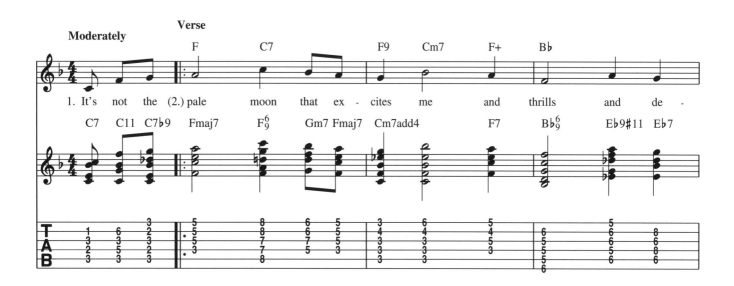

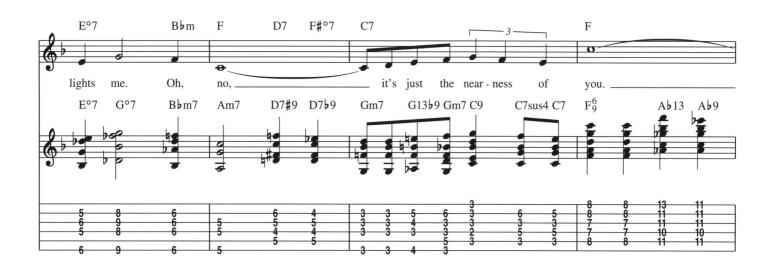

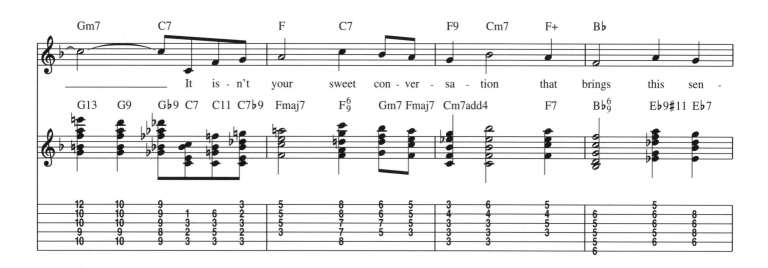

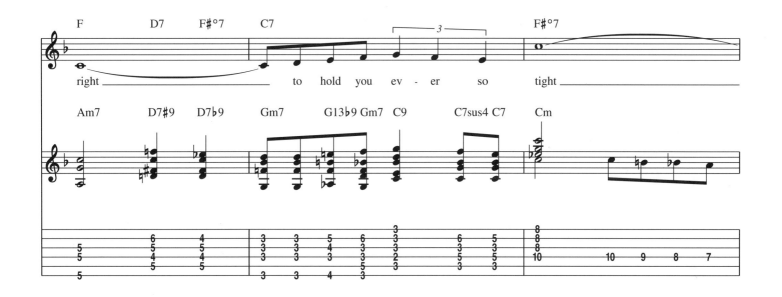

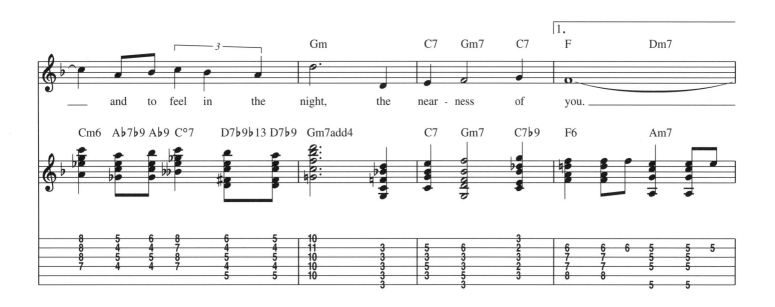

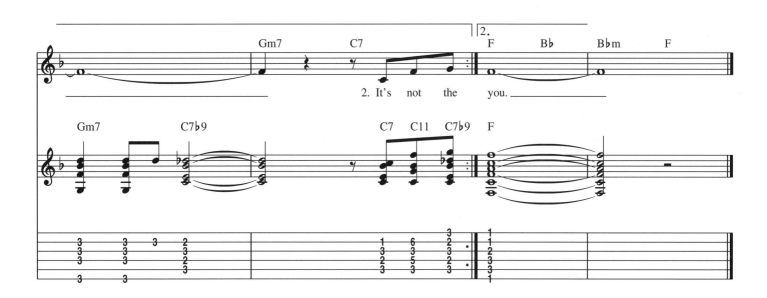

My Funny Valentine

from BABES IN ARMS

Words by Lorenz Hart
Music by Richard Rodgers

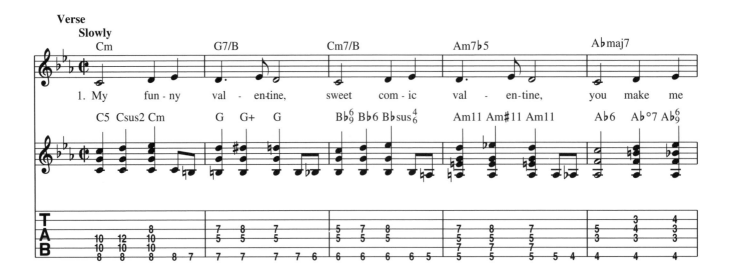

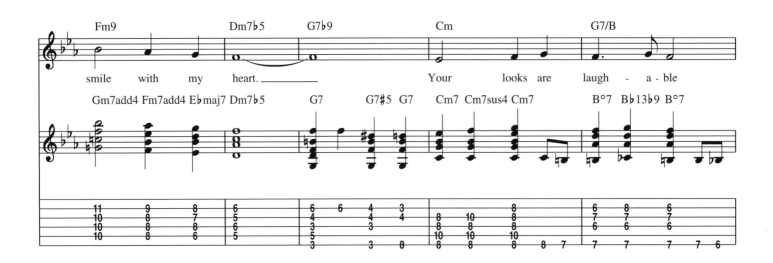

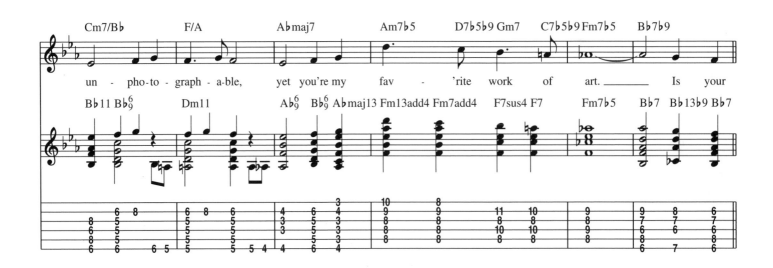

A Nightingale Sang in Berkeley Square

Lyric by Eric Maschwitz
Music by Manning Sherwin

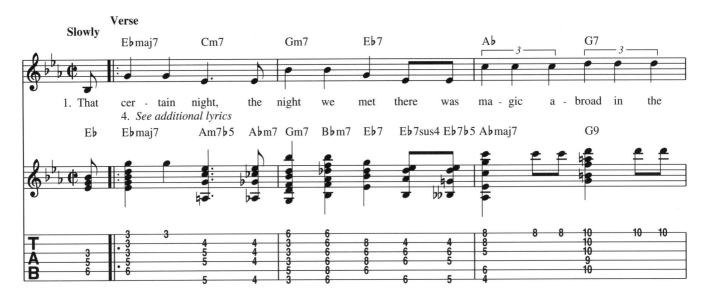

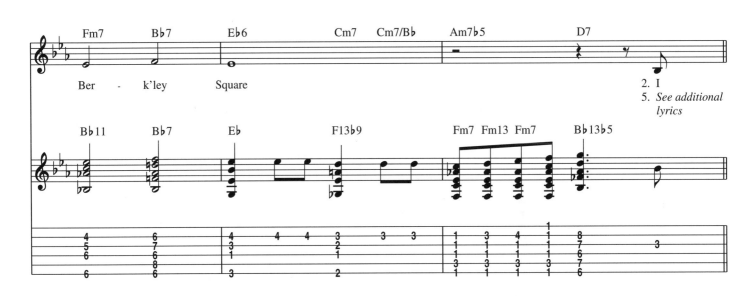

Verse

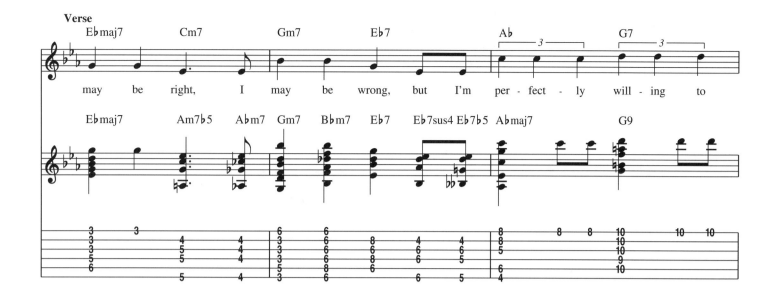

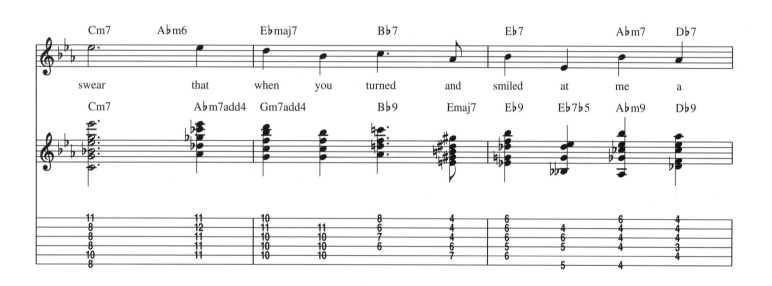

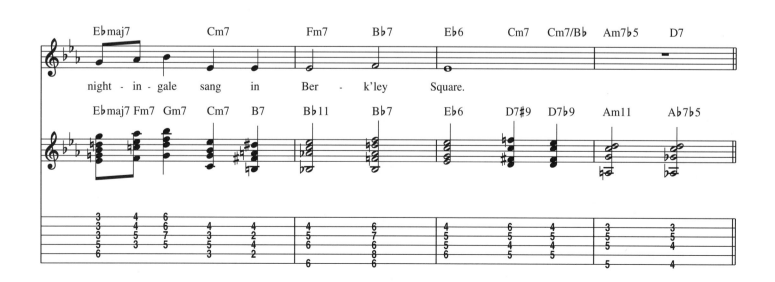

Bridge

The moon that lin - gered o - ver Lon - don town, ___ poor
See additional lyrics

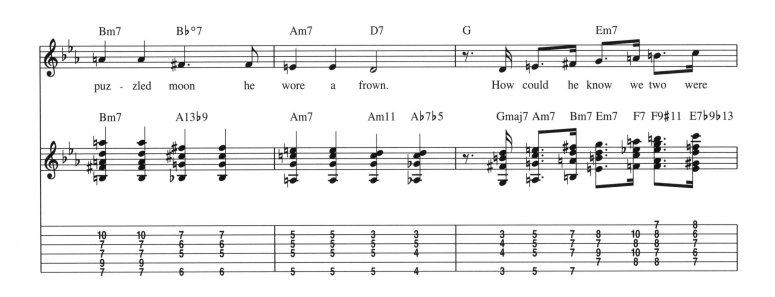

puz - zled moon he wore a frown. How could he know we two were

so in love? _ The whole darn world seemed up - side down. 3. The streets of town were
6. See additional lyrics

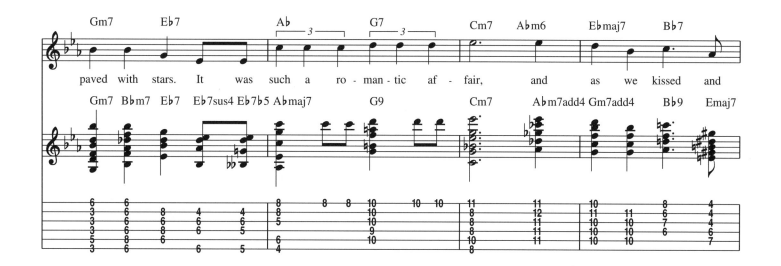

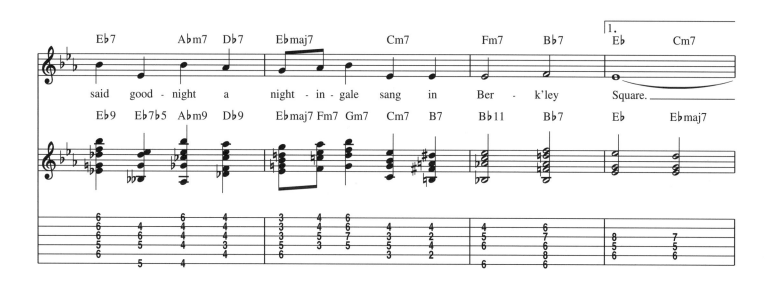

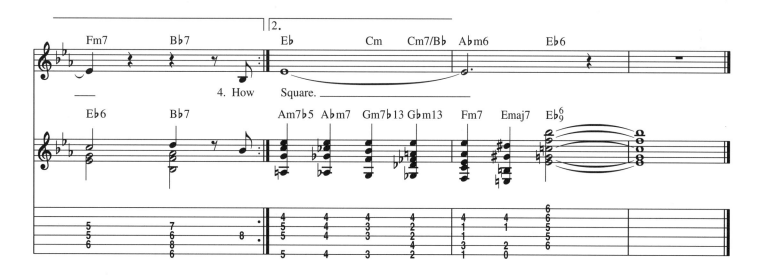

Additional Lyrics

4. How strange it was, how sweet and strange,
   There was never a dream to compare
   With that hazy, crazy night we met,
   When a nightingale sang in Berkley Square.

5. This heart of mine beats loud and fast,
   Like a merry-go-round in a fair,
   For we were dancing cheek to cheek
   And a nightingale sang in Berkeley Square.

Bridge When dawn came stealing up all gold and blue
   To interrupt our rendezvous,
   I still remember how you smiled and said,
   "Was that a dream or was it true?"

6. Our homeward step was just as light
   As the tap-dancing feet of Astaire,
   And like an echo far away
   A nightingale sang in Berkeley Square.

Out of Nowhere

from the Paramount Picture DUDE RANCH

Words by Edward Heyman
Music by Johnny Green

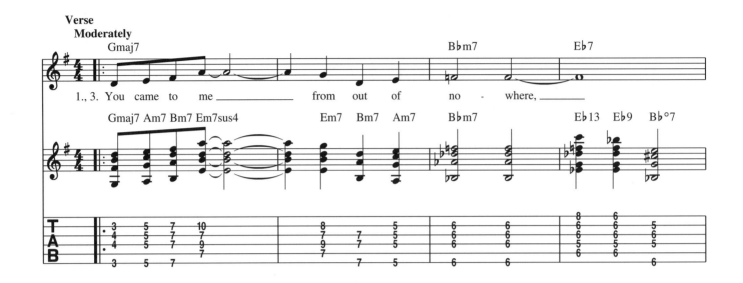

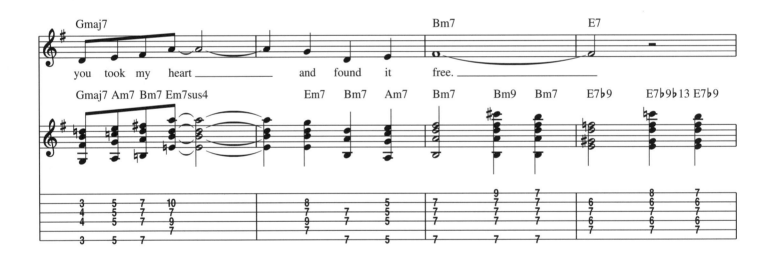

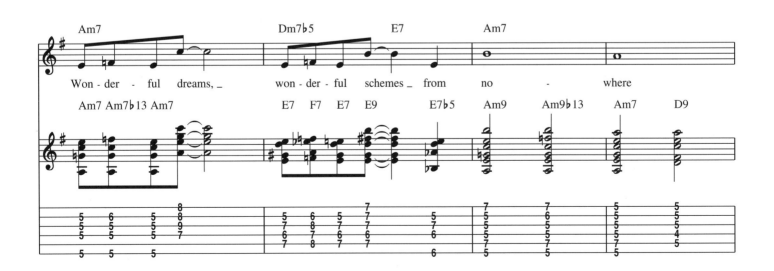

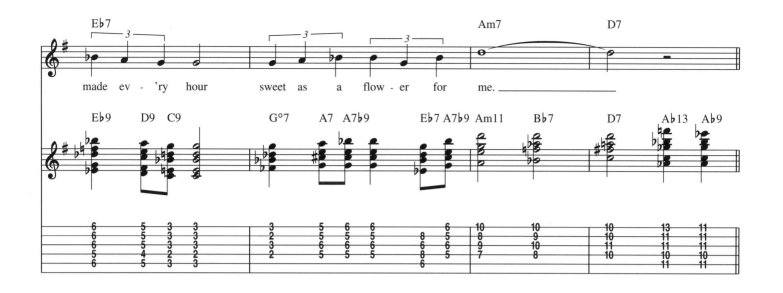

made ev - 'ry hour   sweet as a flow - er   for   me. _____

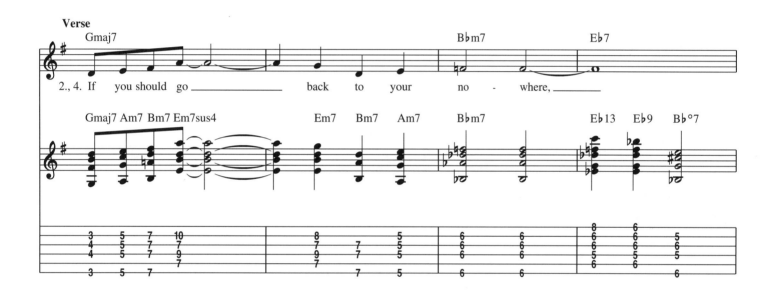

Verse

2., 4. If you should go _____ back to your no - where, _____

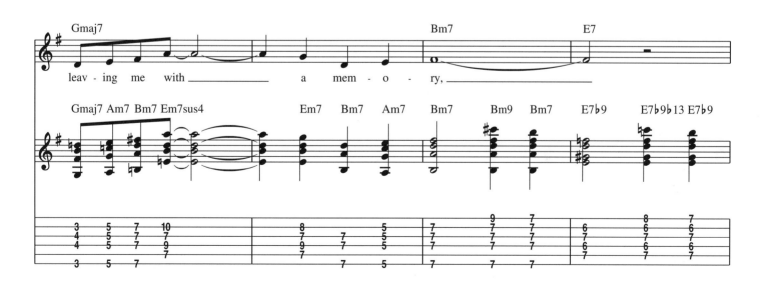

leav - ing me with _____ a mem - o - ry, _____

I'll al - ways wait ___ for your re - turn out of no -

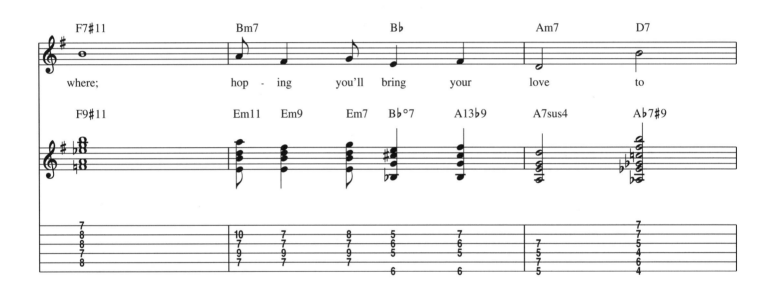

where; hop - ing you'll bring your love to

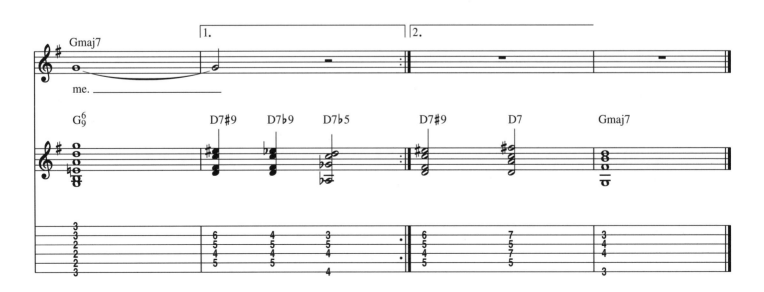

me. ___

Prelude to a Kiss

Words by Irving Gordon and Irving Mills
Music by Duke Ellington

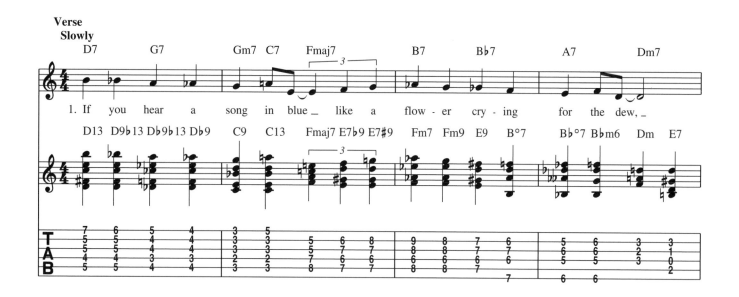

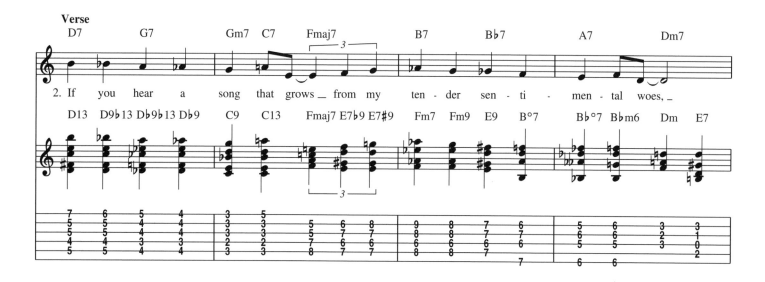

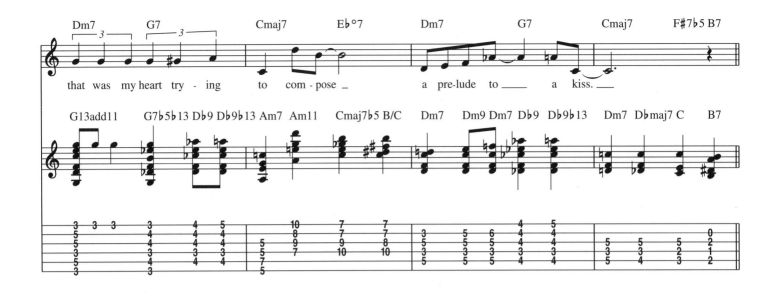

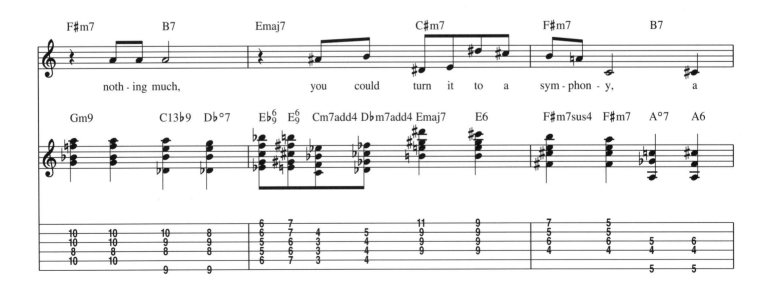

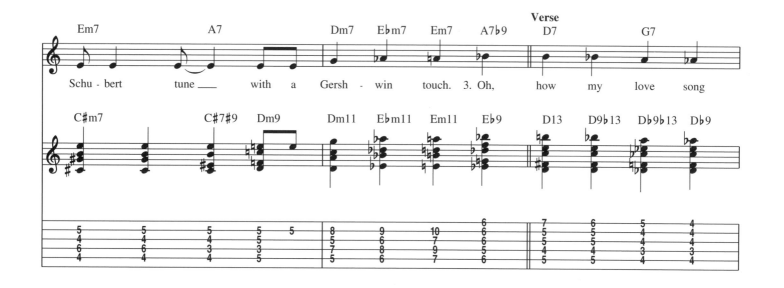

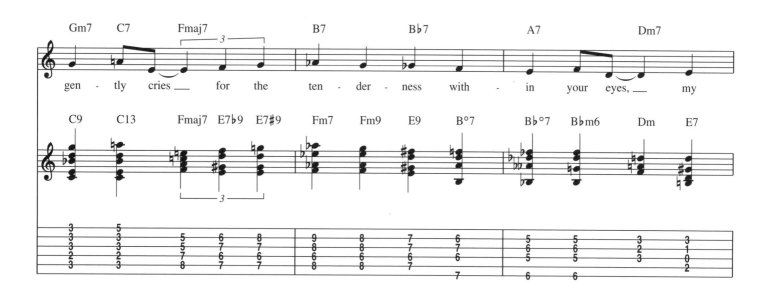

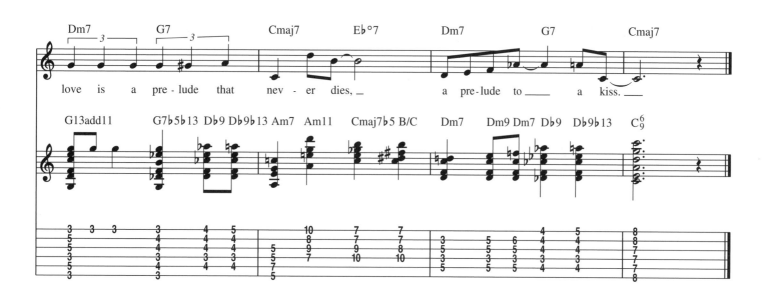

Slightly Out of Tune
(Desafinado)

English Lyric by Jon Hendricks and Jessie Cavanaugh
Original Text by Newton Mendonca
Music by Antonio Carlos Jobim

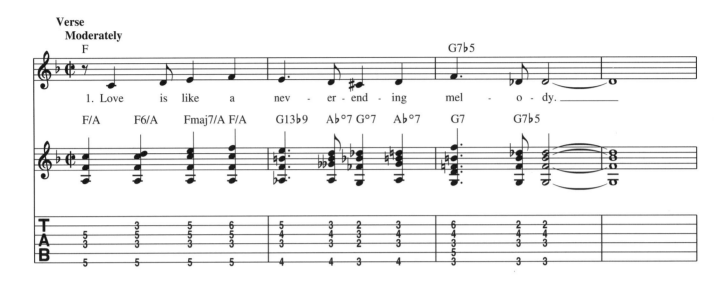

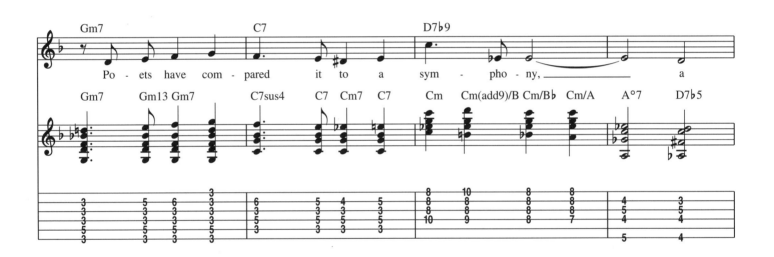

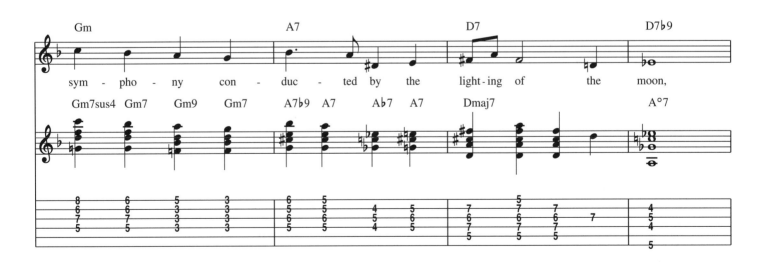

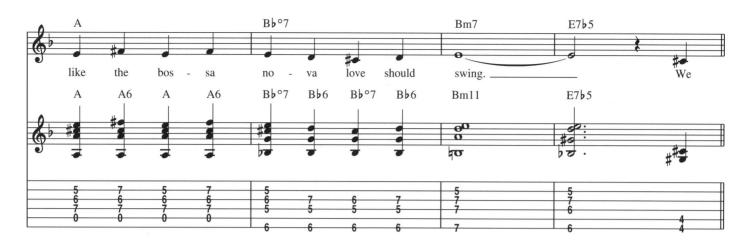

like the bos-sa no-va love should swing. _____ We

Bridge

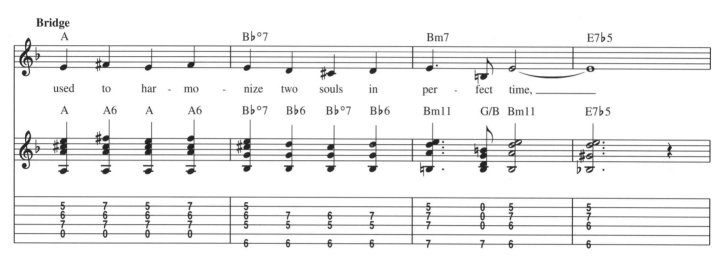

used to har - mo - nize two souls in per - fect time, _____

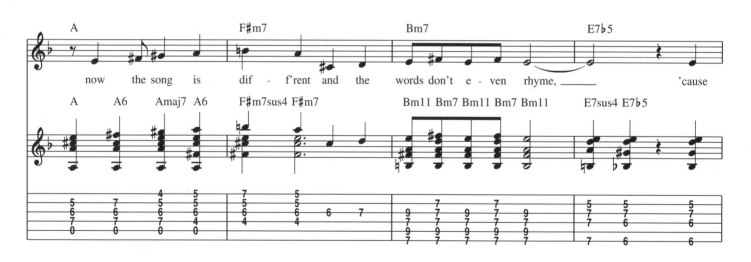

now the song is dif - f'rent and the words don't e - ven rhyme, _____ 'cause

you for - got the mel - o - dy our hearts would al - ways croon. ____ And so what

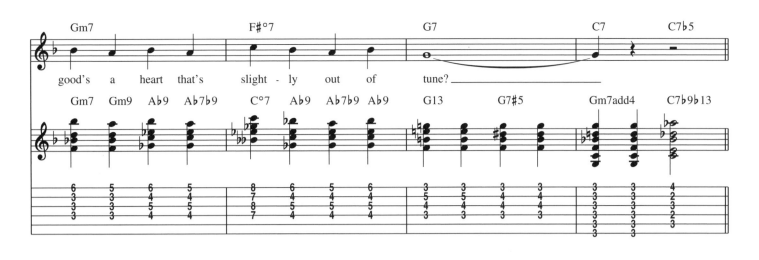

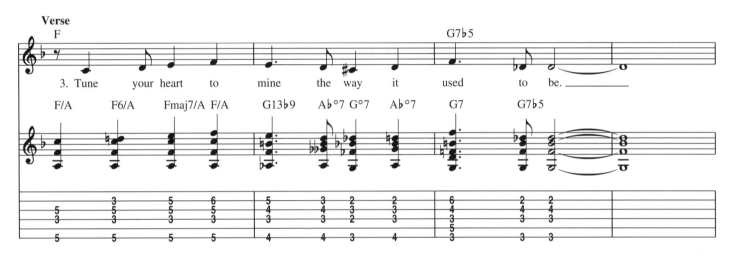

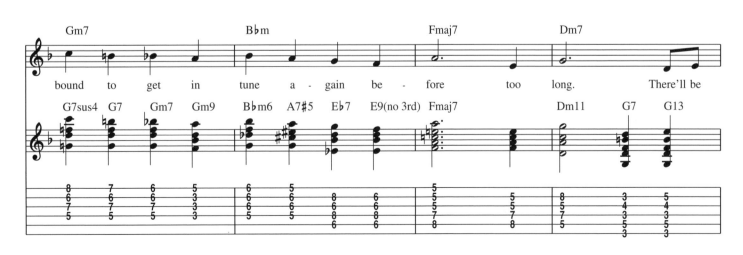

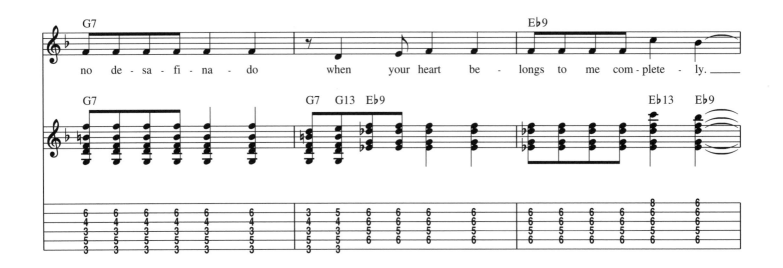

no de - sa - fi - na - do   when your heart be - longs to me com - plete - ly. _____

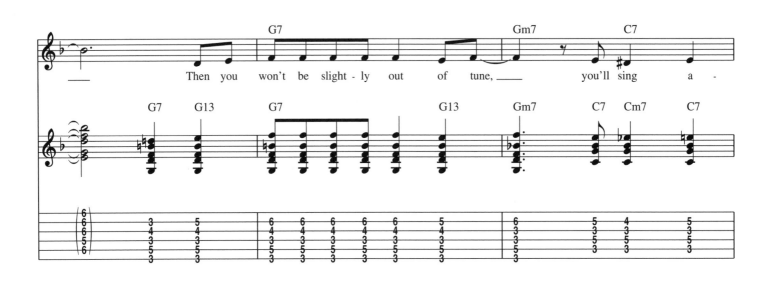

_____   Then you won't be slight - ly out of tune, _____ you'll sing a -

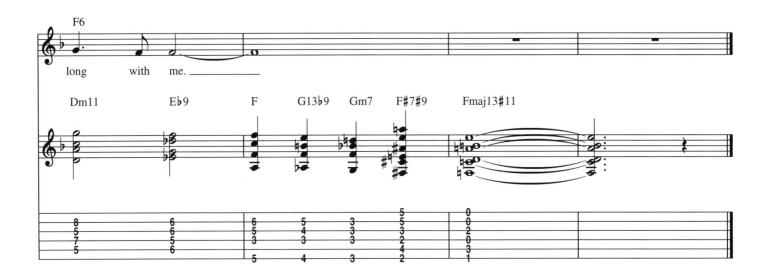

long   with   me. _____

Softly As in a Morning Sunrise

from THE NEW MOON

Lyrics by Oscar Hammerstein II
Music by Sigmund Romberg

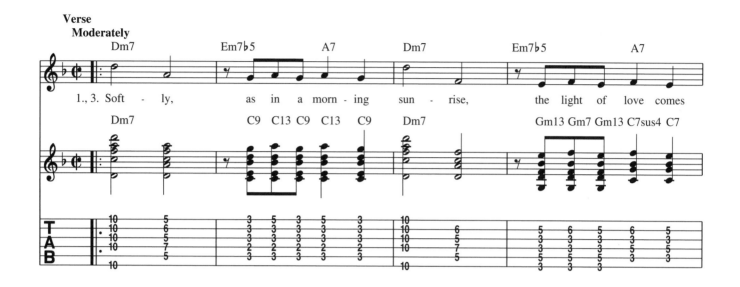

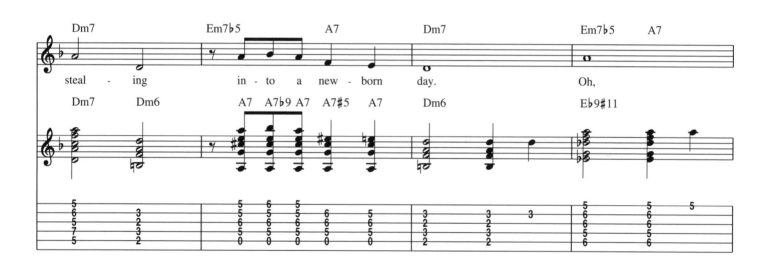

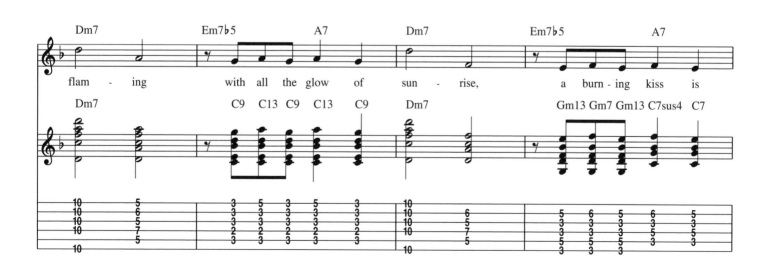

seal - ing the vow that all be - tray. For the pas - sions that

Bridge

thrill love, and lift you high to heav - en, _____ are the pas - sions that

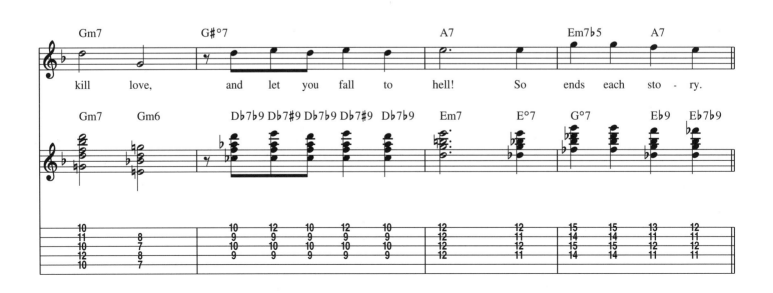

kill love, and let you fall to hell! So ends each sto - ry.

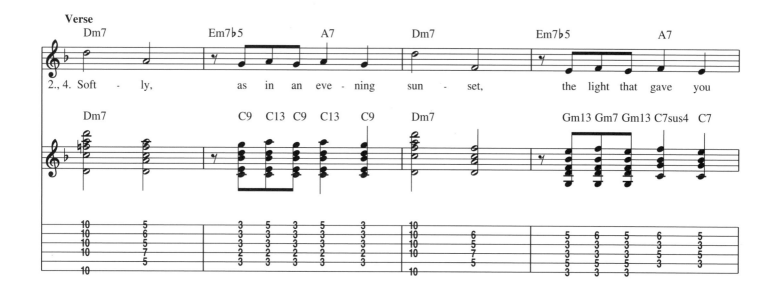

2., 4. Soft - ly,   as in an eve - ning sun - set,   the light that gave you

glo - ry   will take it all a - way.

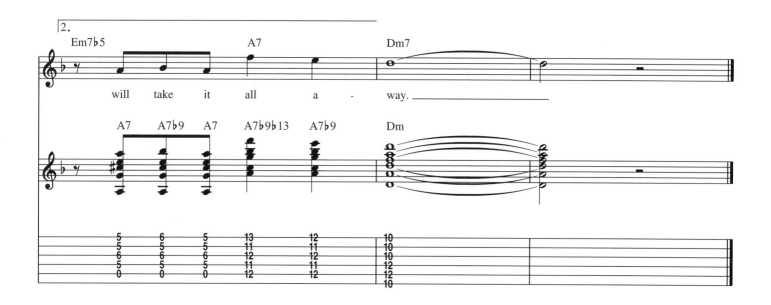

will take it all a - way.

Stella by Starlight

from the Paramount Picture THE UNINVITED

Words by Ned Washington
Music by Victor Young

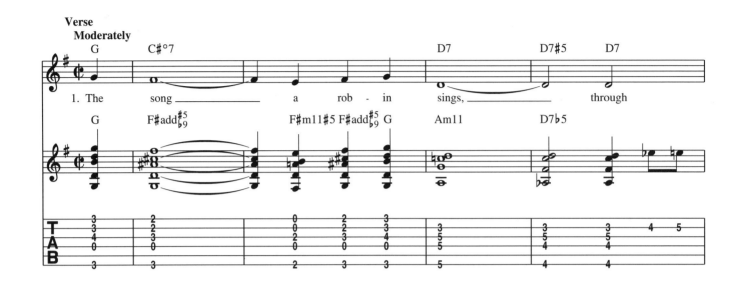

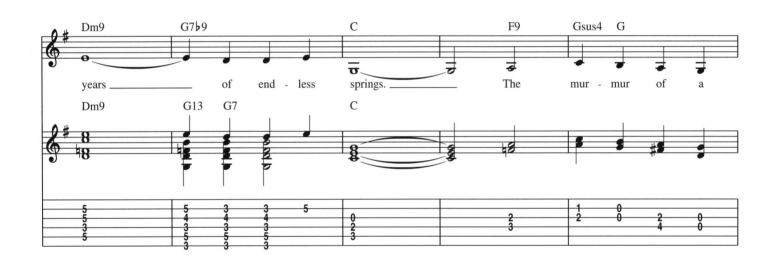

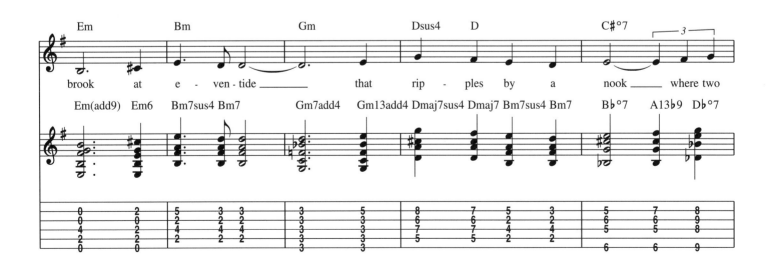

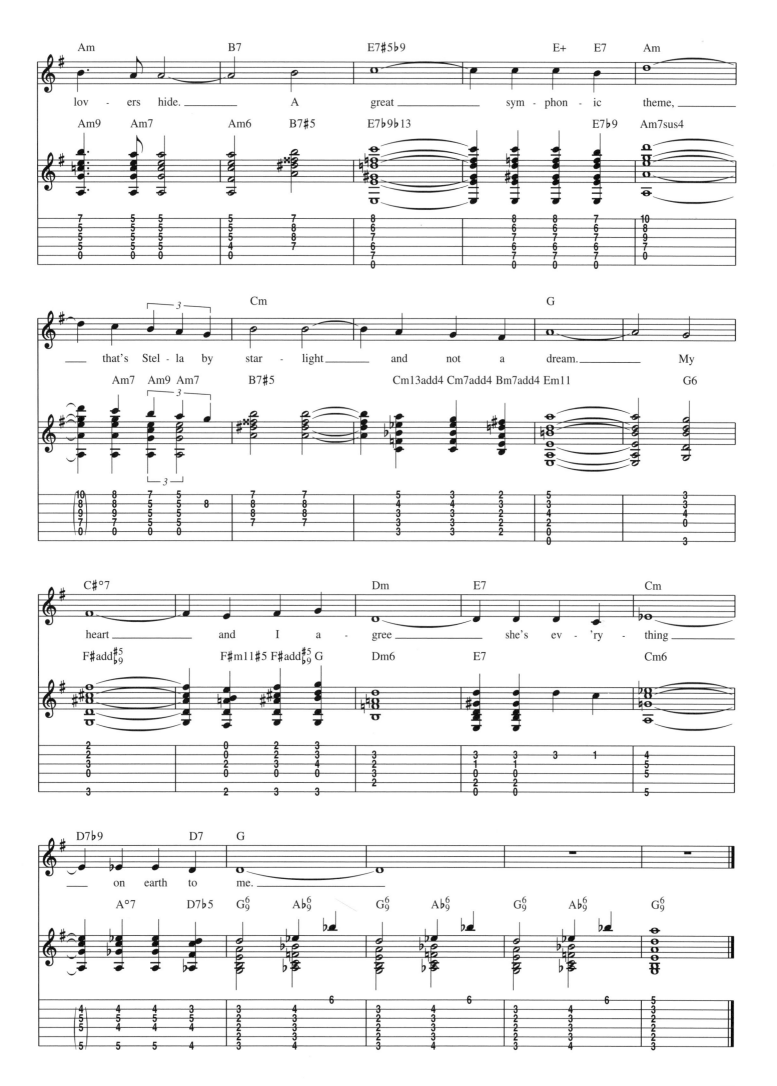

Tangerine

from the Paramount Picture THE FLEET'S IN

Words by Johnny Mercer
Music by Victor Schertzinger

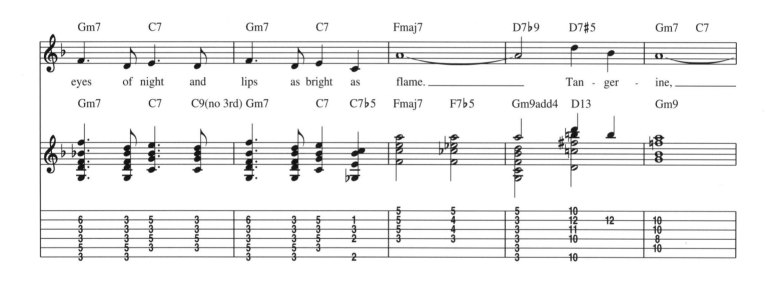

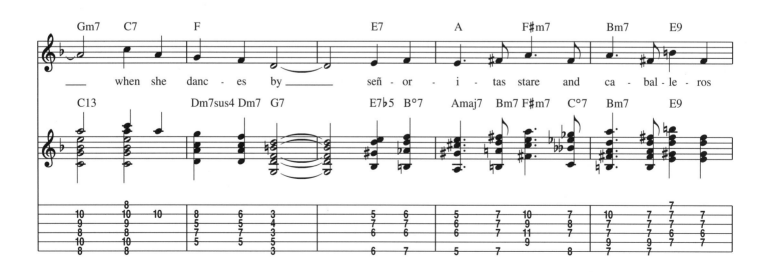

There Will Never Be Another You

from the Motion Picture ICELAND

Lyric by Mack Gordon
Music by Harry Warren

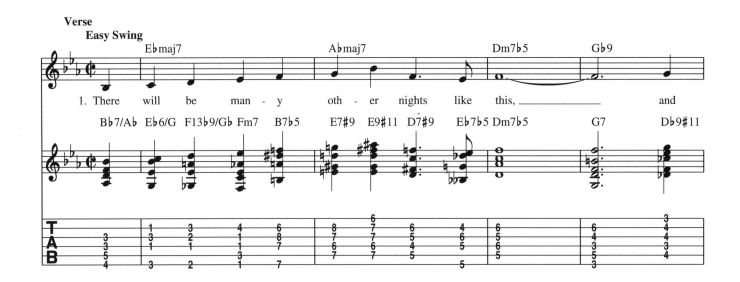

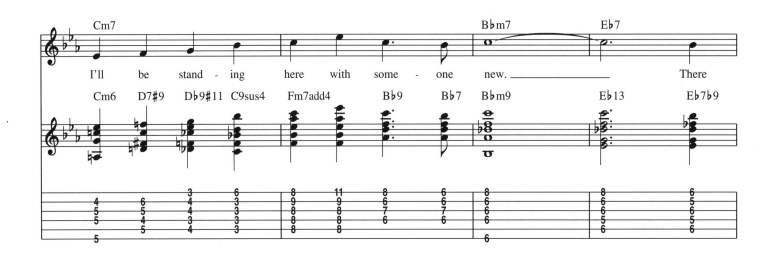

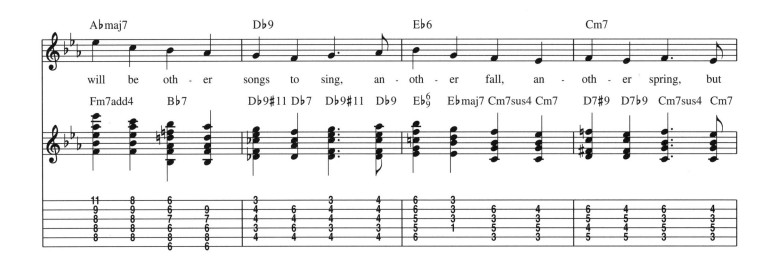

there will nev - er be an - oth - er you. _____ 2. There

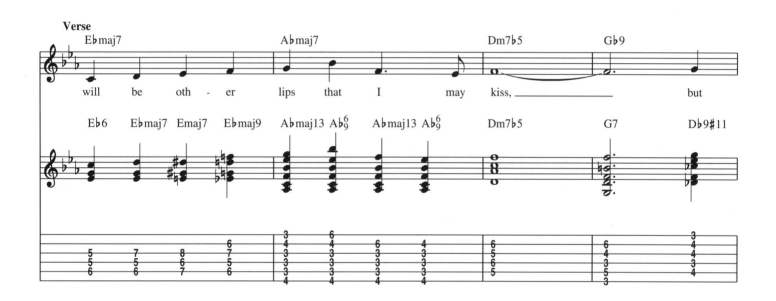

Verse

will be oth - er lips that I may kiss, _____ but

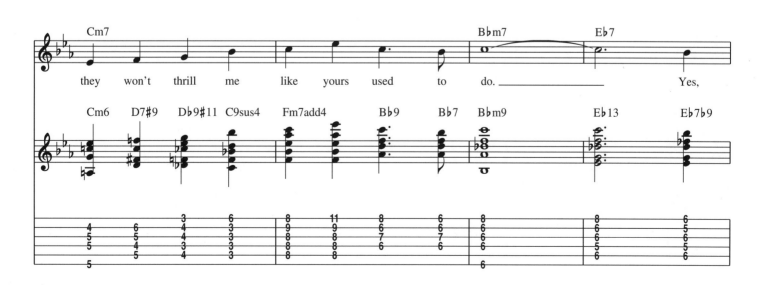

they won't thrill me like yours used to do. _____ Yes,

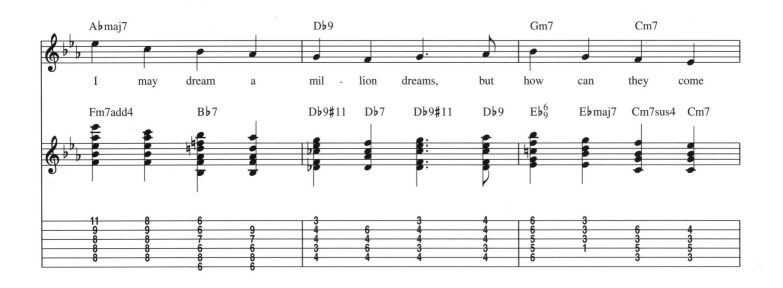

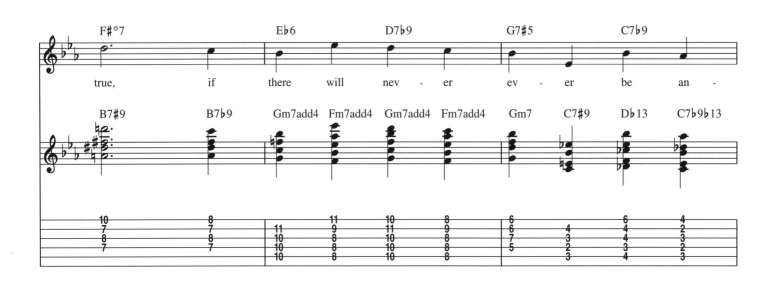

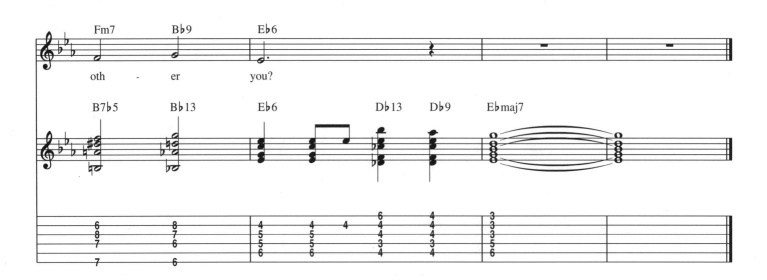

The Very Thought of You

Words and Music by Ray Noble

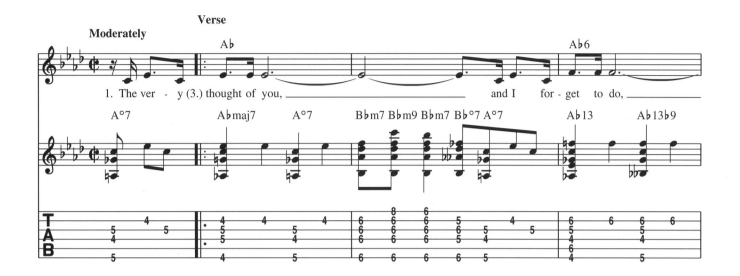

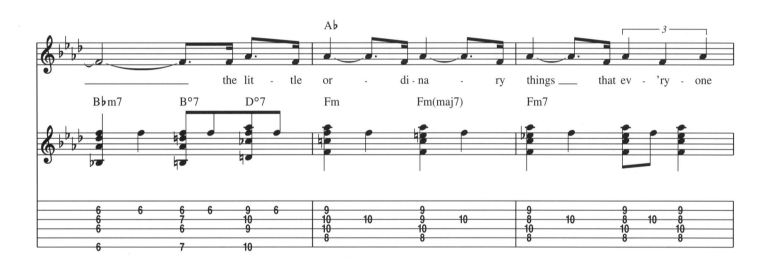

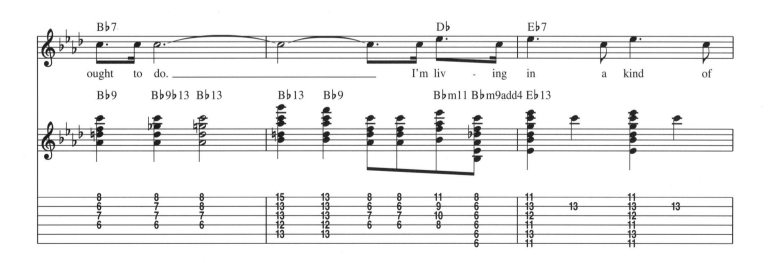

This Can't Be Love

from THE BOYS FROM SYRACUSE

Words by Lorenz Hart
Music by Richard Rodgers

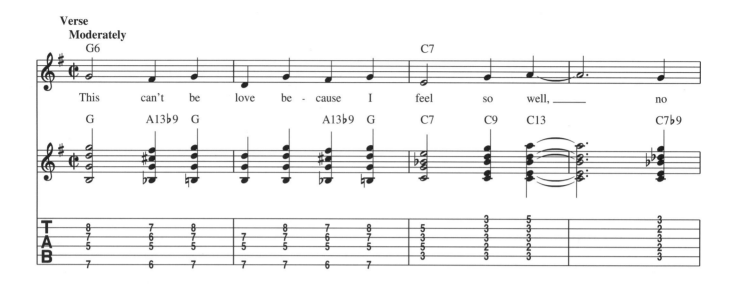

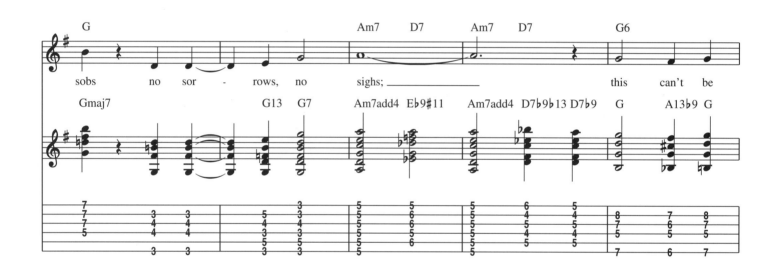

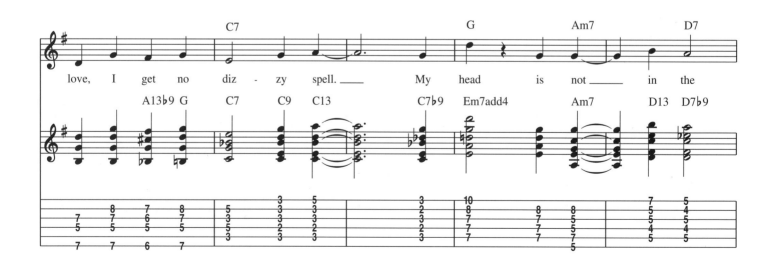

When Sunny Gets Blue

Lyric by Jack Segal
Music by Marvin Fisher

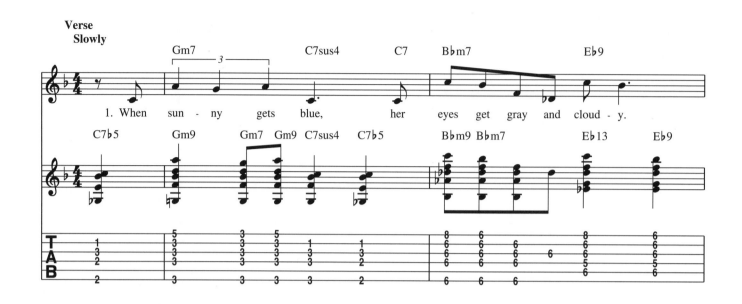

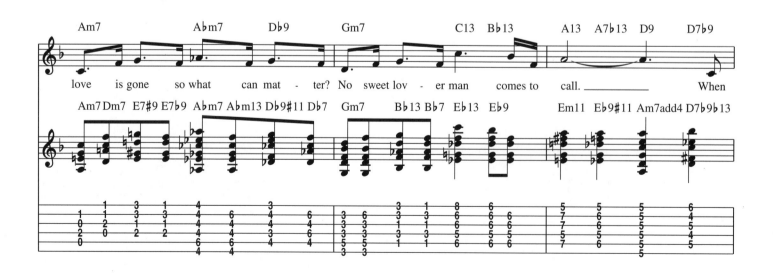

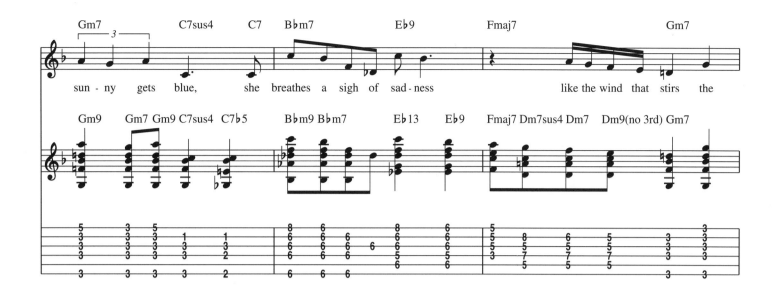

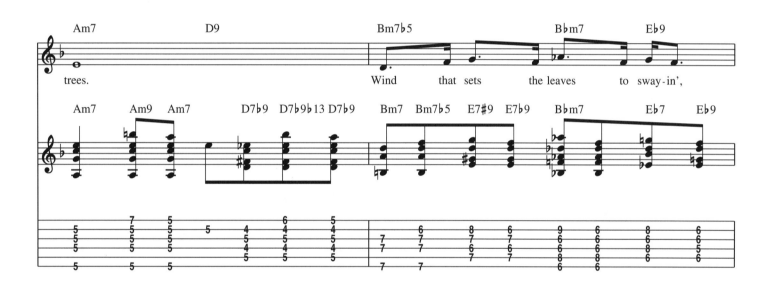

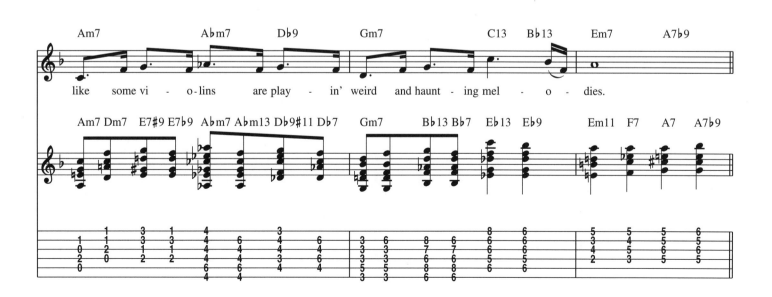

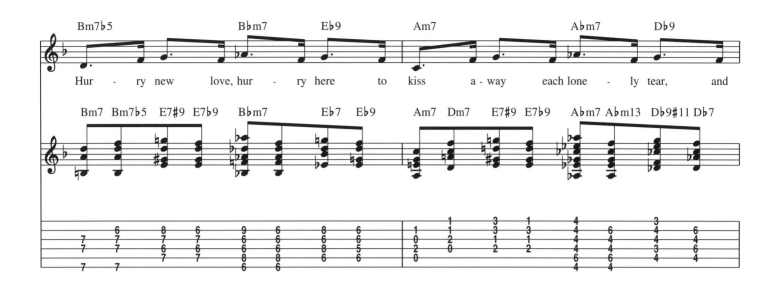

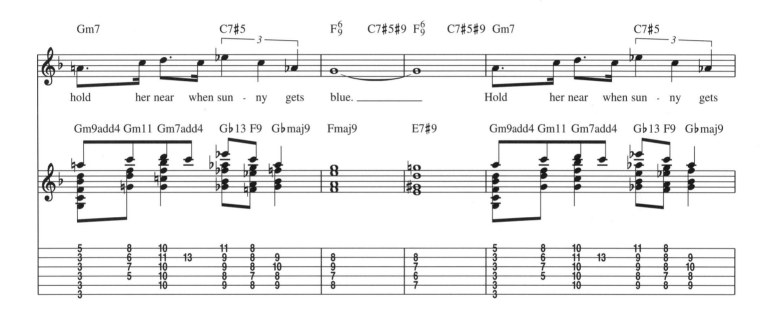

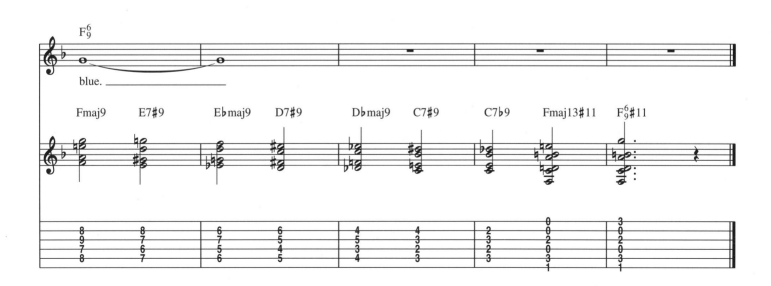

Yesterday

Words and Music by John Lennon and Paul McCartney

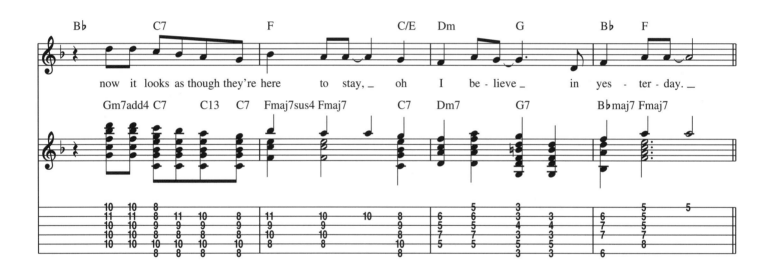

there's a shad-ow hang-ing o - ver me, __ oh yes - ter-day __ came sud - den - ly. __

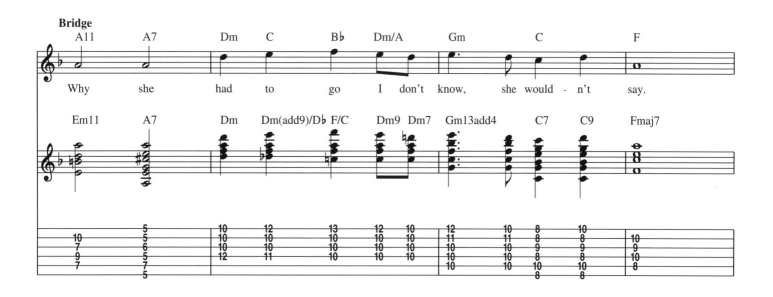

Bridge

Why she had to go I don't know, she would - n't say.

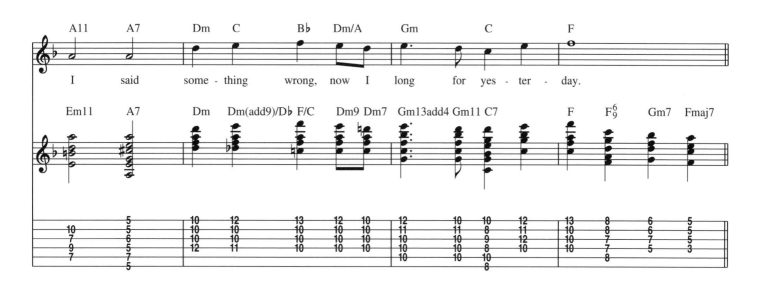

I said some - thing wrong, now I long for yes - ter - day.

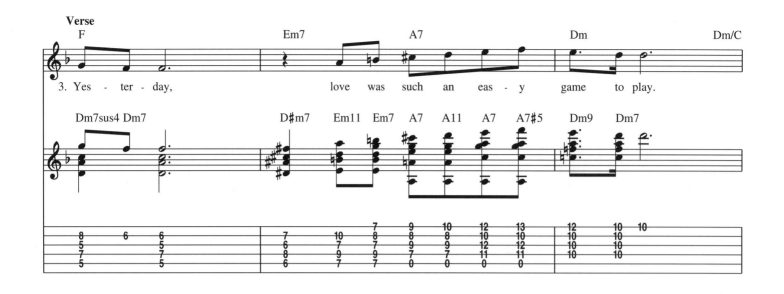

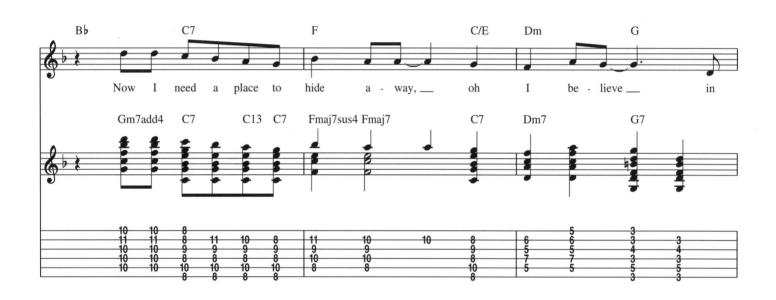

Verse
F Em7 A7 Dm Dm/C
3. Yes - ter - day, love was such an eas - y game to play.
Dm7sus4 Dm7 D♯m7 Em11 Em7 A7 A11 A7 A7♯5 Dm9 Dm7
B♭ C7 F C/E Dm G
Now I need a place to hide a - way, oh I be - lieve in
Gm7add4 C7 C13 C7 Fmaj7sus4 Fmaj7 C7 Dm7 G7
B♭ F Dm G B♭ F
yes - ter - day. Mm, mm, mm, mm, mm.
B♭maj7 Fmaj7 Dm7 G7 B♭maj7 G♭maj7 Fmaj7

ABOUT THE AUTHOR

Robert Yelin is a guitarist, arranger, educator, and writer who has been playing jazz for over 40 years. His first inspiration came from Johnny Smith's chord-melody solos, and it was the rich variety of guitar chords that moved him to arrange nearly 2,000 songs to date. His 1982 album *Night Rain* was named best solo instrumental album in *Cadence* magazine's critics poll. *Guitar Player* wrote: "Yelin's arrangements are unique. He looks for the right chord; not the right lick. He uses alternate tunings, harmonics, and pizzicato effects tastefully while he whips through difficult passages with no sense of strain." In the liner notes for Yelin's jazz trio album *Song For My Wife*, Johnny Smith wrote: "Bob Yelin is an excellent jazz guitarist and this is an excellent album. His music leaves a lasting, musical memory."

In addition to leading the jazz guitar ensemble at the University of Colorado, Bob Yelin has had over 3,500 private students. For more than 20 years he has taught improvisation and chords through his correspondence course. He was *Guitar Player's* contributing jazz editor from 1968-1982, and his writings have also appeared in *Frets* and *Just Jazz Guitar* magazines. His bio can be found in *Who's Who in Entertainment* and the highly respected book, *The Jazz Guitar — It's Evolution, Players and Personalities Since 1900*. He has performed throughout the United States as a solo artist and with his jazz trio.

Fellow jazz great Gene Bertoncini may have put it best when he described Bob Yelin and himself as "chordiologists."

Robert Yelin plays 6, 7, and 14 string Buscarino archtop guitars.

Buscarino Guitars
2348 Wide Horizon Drive
Franklin, N.C. 28734
(828) 349-9867

Guitar Notation Legend

Guitar Music can be notated three different ways: on a *musical staff*, in *tablature*, and in *rhythm slashes*.

RHYTHM SLASHES are written above the staff. Strum chords in the rhythm indicated. Use the chord diagrams found at the top of the first page of the transcription for the appropriate chord voicings. Round noteheads indicate single notes.

THE MUSICAL STAFF shows pitches and rhythms and is divided by bar lines into measures. Pitches are named after the first seven letters of the alphabet.

TABLATURE graphically represents the guitar fingerboard. Each horizontal line represents a string, and each number represents a fret.

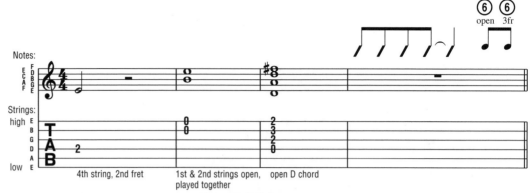

HALF-STEP BEND: Strike the note and bend up 1/2 step.

WHOLE-STEP BEND: Strike the note and bend up one step.

GRACE NOTE BEND: Strike the note and immediately bend up as indicated.

SLIGHT (MICROTONE) BEND: Strike the note and bend up 1/4 step.

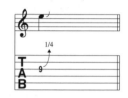

BEND AND RELEASE: Strike the note and bend up as indicated, then release back to the original note. Only the first note is struck.

PRE-BEND: Bend the note as indicated, then strike it.

VIBRATO: The string is vibrated by rapidly bending and releasing the note with the fretting hand.

WIDE VIBRATO: The pitch is varied to a greater degree by vibrating with the fretting hand.

HAMMER-ON: Strike the first (lower) note with one finger, then sound the higher note (on the same string) with another finger by fretting it without picking.

PULL-OFF: Place both fingers on the notes to be sounded. Strike the first note and without picking, pull the finger off to sound the second (lower) note.

LEGATO SLIDE: Strike the first note and then slide the same fret-hand finger up or down to the second note. The second note is not struck.

SHIFT SLIDE: Same as legato slide, except the second note is struck.

TRILL: Very rapidly alternate between the notes indicated by continuously hammering on and pulling off.

TAPPING: Hammer ("tap") the fret indicated with the pick-hand index or middle finger and pull off to the note fretted by the fret hand.

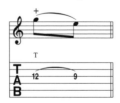

NATURAL HARMONIC: Strike the note while the fret-hand lightly touches the string directly over the fret indicated.

PINCH HARMONIC: The note is fretted normally and a harmonic is produced by adding the edge of the thumb or the tip of the index finger of the pick hand to the normal pick attack.

PICK SCRAPE: The edge of the pick is rubbed down (or up) the string, producing a scratchy sound.

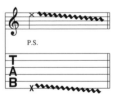

MUFFLED STRINGS: A percussive sound is produced by laying the fret hand across the string(s) without depressing, and striking them with the pick hand.

PALM MUTING: The note is partially muted by the pick hand lightly touching the string(s) just before the bridge.

RAKE: Drag the pick across the strings indicated with a single motion.

TREMOLO PICKING: The note is picked as rapidly and continuously as possible.

VIBRATO BAR DIVE AND RETURN: The pitch of the note or chord is dropped a specified number of steps (in rhythm) then returned to the original pitch.

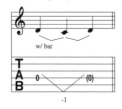

VIBRATO BAR SCOOP: Depress the bar just before striking the note, then quickly release the bar.

VIBRATO BAR DIP: Strike the note and then immediately drop a specified number of steps, then release back to the original pitch.

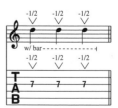